An Introduction To
CIVIL WAR
SMALL ARMS

Earl J. Coates and Dean S. Thomas

CONTENTS

Introduction   3

Springfield Armory   4

Parts of a Rifle Musket   6

Muskets   7

Rifle Muskets   13

Rifles   24

Breechloading Rifles   30

Carbines   36

Revolvers   52

Accoutrements   66

Ammunition   67

Appendages   69

Bayonets   71

Ignition   72

Loading and Firing   75

Glossary   82

Appendices

  A. Federal and Northern State Arsenals   85

  B. Confederate Arsenals, Depots and Laboratories   85

  C. Small Arms Usage by Regiments   86

Bibliography and Suggested Reading   96

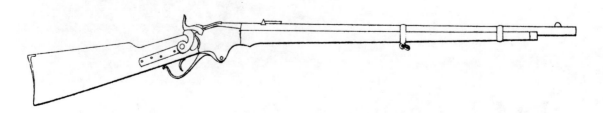

Introduction

Small arms are the firearms carried by individual soldiers. During the American Civil War (1861-65) small arms consisted of an incredible variety of muskets, rifles, carbines, revolvers, and even shotguns. Small arms, in the hands of both Union and Confederate soldiers, accounted for most of the war's 633,000 killed and wounded.

In 1861, neither the United States nor the newly-formed Confederate States were prepared to fight a major war. Years of peace, a small standing army, and a state militia system that was largely ceremonial, combined to severely limit stockpiles of military supplies. The most serious shortage was the lack of up-to-date small arms.

As thousands of volunteers rushed forward to join the armies of the cause in which they believed, the supply of arms in both state and national armories was soon exhausted. To meet the emergency, both Union and Confederate governments sent purchasing agents to scour the arsenals of Europe. Every type of firearm suitable for military purposes was pressed into service in the meantime. Many early volunteers found themselves armed with antiquated weapons, some even dating back to the War of 1812.

The agents operating in Europe wasted little time. By the fall of 1861 ships loaded with European arms and ammunition began to arrive at ports from Boston to New Orleans. In short order, volunteers from such states as New York, Ohio, North Carolina, and Georgia, found themselves armed with weapons originally intended for British, Austrian, Belgian, or French soldiers. As these ships continued to cross the Atlantic, established American arms makers, and those aspiring to be such, rushed to the call.

In the North, well-known arms makers such as Colt, Sharps, and Remington geared for war production. In the South, the Confederate government was attempting to build its own small arms producing facilities. This ambitious goal was a necessity if it was ever to lessen reliance on imported weapons. Unfortunately for the South, this goal was never fully attained.

In 1862 and 1863 Southern industry did make amazing strides in its ability to provide conventional muzzleloading arms to Southern soldiers. At the same time, however, this effort was countered by Northern industrial might. Yankee arms makers not only continued to produce conventional arms, but also introduced a number of technically advanced small arms which would begin to revolutionize warfare. By 1865, one such arm, the magazine-fed breechloading Spencer carbine gained world wide attention.

Early Southern victories provided many Confederate soldiers with Federal arms. Capture and battlefield pick-up of small arms remained an important supply source for the South until the last days of the conflict. Thus, many weapons which were only manufactured in the North also served the Southern cause. Capture was also a source of supply to some Union troops. Many who were initially armed with substandard or antiquated arms acquired British Enfields and other quality foreign weapons from Confederate prisoners or casualties.

The story of Civil War small arms is as colorful and varied as that of the men who carried them. It is the intention of this volume to provide the reader with an accurate overview of this fascinating segment of our Nation's history.

Not all Civil War small arms are listed here, but all of the major types and many of the minor types are included. Arms and the men who carried them are historically inseparable. Because of this, an effort has been made to photographically reunite some of those who carried these weapons with the story of the arms themselves.

Small arms are worthless without ammunition. For this reason, the often unique types of cartridges are also shown with the arms in which they were used.

A glossary is provided to familiarize the reader with Civil War small arms terminology. A suggested reading list is also supplied to assist those who wish to pursue the subject in greater detail.

It is hoped that the regimental listings to be found in Appendix C will provide a handy reference to many who are interested in the arms carried by specific regiments.

The reader will notice that several descriptions are without an accompanying photograph of a soldier carrying the weapon. The authors made every attempt to locate photographs of every arm in use by the soldiers, but were sometimes unable to do so. If any readers are aware of photographs which could be added to future editions, please contact Thomas Publications. Any photographs supplied to us and used in a future edition will be acknowledged in print.

Springfield Armory and Small Arms Production

By 1861, the United States was in the middle of an industrial revolution. Mass production was beginning to leave its indelible mark on American society. Using the concept of interchangeable parts pioneered by such men as Eli Whitney, intricate mechanical devices were becoming affordable to the average American. An excellent example was the Singer sewing machine which could be found in many American homes. But in 1861 the nation's industrial force changed its emphasis from tools of peace to weapons of war.

The United States armory, located at Springfield, Massachusetts, had been a leader in applying automation to production since the late 1840s. Although some hand assembly of arms was still necessary, the majority of the preassembly work was done by skilled craftsmen operating sophisticated machines.

Machine production allowed the simultaneous manufacture of identical and fully interchangeable parts. Total interchangeability eliminated costly hand-fitting of each part. The production rate thus took a quantum step forward. During 1863 Springfield was able to turn out an average of 600 rifle-muskets a day. During the period of the Civil War, this single location placed 797,936 first class rifle-muskets in the hands of the Union army.

To a large extent, machine capability was in practice at every arms producing facility in the north. The ability to manufacture intricate interchangeable parts also influenced the type of arms produced by them. Complex magazine-fed rifles such as the Henry and Spencer showed the world what American ingenuity could do.

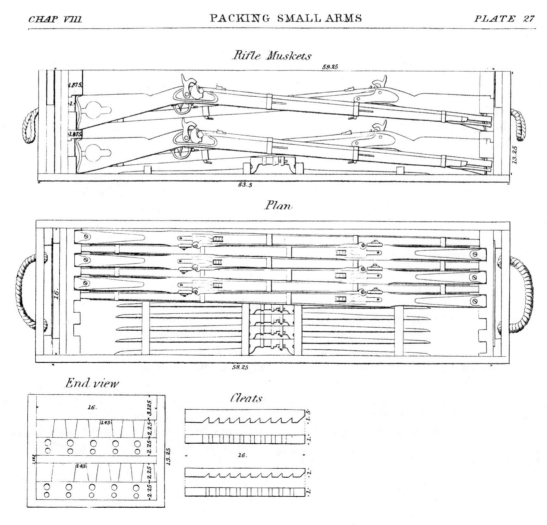

CHAP VIII PACKING SMALL ARMS *PLATE 27*

Rifle Muskets

Plan

End view *Cleats*

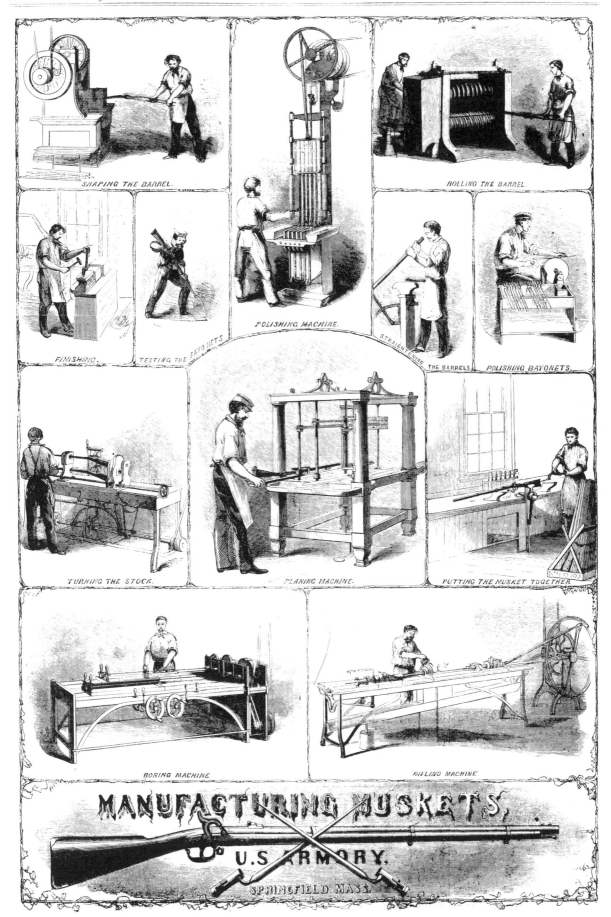

SHAPING THE BARREL.

ROLLING THE BARREL.

FINISHING.

TESTING THE BAYONETS.

POLISHING MACHINE.

STRAIGHTENING THE BARRELS.

POLISHING BAYONETS.

TURNING THE STOCK.

PLANING MACHINE.

PUTTING THE MUSKET TOGETHER.

BORING MACHINE.

RIFLING MACHINE.

MANUFACTURING MUSKETS, U.S. ARMORY, SPRINGFIELD MASS.

Parts of a Rifle Musket

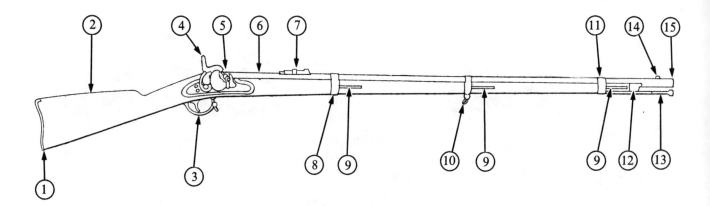

1. Butt and Butt Plate
2. Stock (wood, usually walnut)
3. Trigger and Trigger Guard with Sling Swivel
4. Hammer and Lock
5. Cone
6. Barrel
7. Rear Sight
8. Rear Barrel Band

9. Bandsprings
10. Middle Barrel Band with Sling Swivel
11. Front Barrel Band
12. Nose Cap
13. Ramrod
14. Front Sight
15. Muzzle

Parts of the Model 1855 Lock

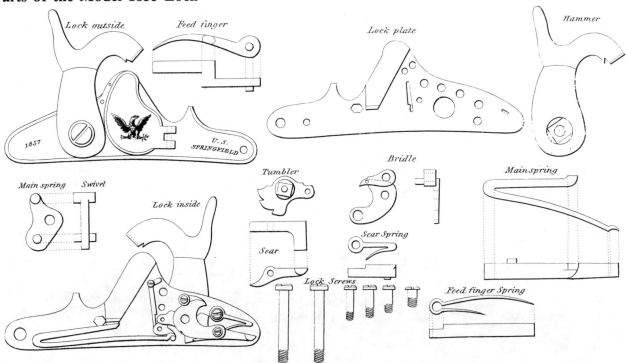

MUSKETS

Model 1816 Musket

Model 1816 Conversion

Model 1842 Musket and

    Model 1842 Rifle Musket

Model 1842 "Palmetto" Musket

Model 1816 Musket

Specifications

Length: 56.75''

Weight: about 9 lbs.

Caliber: .69

Bayonet: angular

The model 1816 musket was one of the oldest arms to see extensive combat use in the Civil War. The model 1816 was produced from its inception until 1840 at both the Harpers Ferry and Springfield Armories, as well as by several contractors. During this time well over 800,000 were manufactured.

The 1816 was the last U.S. arm to be made using the old flint-lock ignition system. This system employed a piece of flint clamped into the top of the musket hammer. When fired, the hammer fell forward, causing the flint to strike a spring-held vertical piece of steel called a frizzen. As the frizzen snapped back the resulting sparks were forced downward to a priming charge of gunpowder. The ignition of this powder passed fire through a pin-sized hole and ignited the powder charge. The advent of the small brass percussion cap in the 1830s, with its self-contained explosive charge, eliminated the need for flint, frizzen, and priming powder and thus made flint-lock arms obsolete. But because of the large number of model 1816 muskets produced, the arm was widely used by state militia units in the 1840s and 1850s. Many of these arms were converted by the states to the newer percussion ignition system, but in 1861 many still retained the original flint-lock.

Many volunteers of 1861 from both the North and South found themselves armed with the 1816 musket. These men carried their vintage arms until, either through regular issue or the fortunes of war, they could be replaced by more modern weapons. By 1863, few model 1816 muskets remained in active service.

Remington Conversion of the Model 1816 Musket

In 1855 the Remington Arms Company received a contract to modernize 20,000 model 1816 muskets. This modernization consisted of the total replacement of the flint-lock and the conversion of the barrel breech to a percussion ignition system. The lock selected was a Remington-made model of the Maynard tape primer. This was the same basic style of lock found on the new 1855 model rifle musket which was then being produced to arm the Regular Army. The work was completed by 1858.

In just three years these arms were needed. They were nearly all issued to the early volunteers. Like the other arms that employed the Maynard tape system, the tape itself found little use in combat. The arms themselves, however, with the standard percussion cap, saw heavy use in 1861 and 1862.

Specifications

Length: 56.75''

Weight: about 9 lbs.

Caliber: .69

Bayonet: angular

M1816 percussion conversions, Remington's at left.

Model 1842 Musket

Specifications

Length: 57.75"

Weight: about 9 lbs.

Caliber: .69

Bayonet: angular

The model 1842 musket was produced by both the Springfield, Massachusetts and Harpers Ferry, Virginia armories. This was the first U.S. musket that used the percussion cap ignition system. Approximately 250,000 arms of model 1842 were produced from 1844 to 1855.

The model 1842 was the standard arm of the U.S. infantry prior to 1855. At the outbreak of the Civil War thousands of these arms were stored in U.S. and state arsenals. Additional thousands were in the hands of state militia units. As a result of this, the model 1842 saw extensive Civil War action, especially in the first two years of the war. Many volunteer regiments from both the North and South still carried this weapon into battle at Gettysburg in 1863.

Model 1842 Rifle Musket

Specifications

Length: 57.75''

Weight: about 9 lbs.

Caliber: .69

Bayonet: angular

The adoption of the rifle musket by the U.S. Army in 1855 made the smooth-bore model 1842 obsolete. At that time, those in the hands of the Federal government were returned to the arsenals and the barrels were rifled. As with most smoothbore arms, the original model 1842 had no rear sight. The additional range and accuracy gained by rifling made a rear sight desirable; many were added to government arms at this time.

Model 1842 "Palmetto" Musket

Specifications

Length: 57.5''

Weight: about 9 lbs.

Caliber: .69

Bayonet: angular

The model 1842 "Palmetto" musket was produced in the early 1850s by Wm. Glaze & Co. of Columbia, South Carolina. These arms were nearly an exact duplicate of the U.S. model 1842 percussion musket. The most noticeable deviation was the barrel bands which were usually brass rather than iron. About 6,000 of these well made weapons were produced for the state of South Carolina. The lock plates on these muskets showed clearly their Southern heritage. Forward of the hammer was neatly stamped a Palmetto tree (hence its nickname) surrounded by the words "Palmetto Armory S*C." To the rear of the hammer was found "Columbia, S.C." and the date.

In 1861, most, if not all of these arms were in the hands of the South Carolina militia. These troops were among the earliest Confederate volunteers. When they left for war, their "Palmetto" muskets went with them.

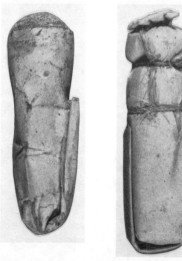

Confederate-made cartridges for .69 cal. smoothbores: round shot by Selma (left) and buck & ball by Richmond (right).

RIFLE MUSKETS

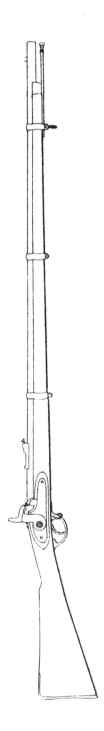

Model 1855 Rifle Musket

Model 1861 Rifle Musket

Special Model 1861 and

      Model 1863 Rifle Muskets

British Pattern '53 "Enfield" Rifle Musket

C.S. Richmond Rifle Musket

Austrian "Lorenz" Rifle Musket

Belgian and French Rifle Muskets

"Dresden" Rifle Muskets

Model 1855 Rifle Musket and Model 1855 Rifle

Specifications

Length: 56''

Weight: about 9 lbs.

Caliber: .58

Bayonet: angular

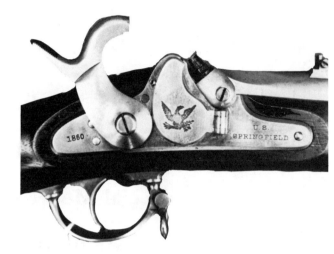

The model 1855 rifle musket has the distinction of being the first rifle musket produced by the United States. The 1855 was manufactured at both government armories: Springfield, Massachusetts and Harpers Ferry, Virginia.

In addition, the 1855 was also the first U.S. arm to fire the famed .58 cal. Minie ball. A distinctive feature of this weapon was the lock which contains a Maynard tape primer system. This innovative mechanism eliminated the need for a percussion cap by substituting a roll of caps nearly identical to those used in 20th century toy cap pistols. By cocking the hammer, a cap was fed out and over the nipple. When the trigger was pulled, causing the hammer to fall, the cap was forced onto the nipple and the resulting explosion fired the arm. A second distinctive feature of the model 1855 produced from 1859 to 1861 was the inclusion of a sporting type patch box in the butt stock.

A shorter version of the 1855 rifle musket, termed the model 1855 rifle, was produced at the Harpers Ferry Armory from 1857 to 1861. Just over 7,000 1855 rifles were produced, many of which had a special long range rear sight which allowed sighting up to 400 yards.

Although a few elite state militia units were armed with the 1855 rifle musket, they were primarily the arm of the regular infantry. When Confederate forces seized the U.S. Armory at Harpers Ferry in 1861, they took machinery used to produce the 1855's. In the same year Springfield ceased production of this arm in favor of the model 1861 rifle musket.

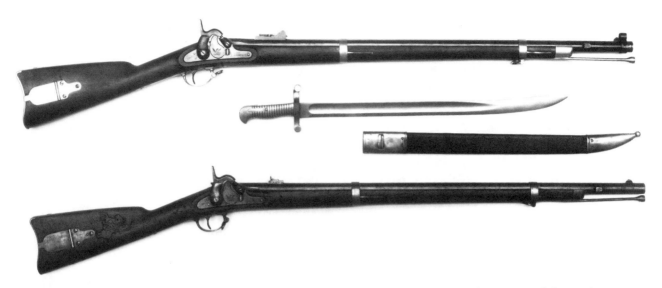

M1855 rifles with sword bayonet and scabbard, Type I - brass mounted (top) and Type II - iron mounted (bottom).

Model 1861 Rifle Musket

Specifications

Length: 56''

Weight: about 9 lbs.

Caliber: .58

Bayonet: angular

The model 1861 rifle musket was the classic arm of the Civil War infantry soldier. During the war, it was the standard against which all other Civil War shoulder arms were judged. The model 1861 was a refinement of the first United States rifle musket, the model 1855. By elimination of the patch box and the Maynard tape primer the arm was simplified with no loss in quality. This modification had the dual benefits of lowering both the cost and production time of the weapon, critical factors for a nation at war.

The model 1861 was originally manufactured solely at the U.S. Government Armory at Springfield, Massachusetts. The war emergency, however, called for far more arms than could be produced at Springfield. To meet the need, the Ordnance Department found it necessary to contract with 20 separate manufacturers to produce the arm.

The contract-produced model 1861's were identical in nearly every respect to those produced by Springfield. The sole deviation was the contractor's name on the lock-plate instead of that of the National Armory. A total of over 700,000 model 1861 rifle muskets were produced between 1861 and 1865. (see list below)

Regiments receiving the model 1861 considered themselves fortunate. There is no known incident of those so armed exchanging the model 1861 for any other muzzle-loading weapon.

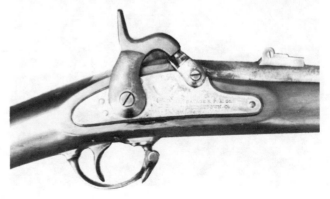

Contractor	Lock marking	No. produced
Alfred Jenks & Son. Bridesburg and Philadelphia, Pa.	U.S.-Bridesburg U.S.-Philadelphia	98,464
Eagle Manufacturing Co. Mansfield, Conn.	U.S.-Eagleville	5,500
William Mason Taunton, Mass.	U.S.-Wm. Mason Taunton	30,000
A.H.Waters & Co. Millbury, Mass.	U.S.-Millbury	not known (very few)
James D. Mowry Norwich, Conn.	U.S.-Jas. D. Mowry Norwich, Conn.	22,000
William Muir & Co. Windsor Locks, Conn.	U.S.-Wm. Muir & Co. Windsor Locks, CT	30,000
Sarson & Roberts New York	U.S. New York	5,140
Welch, Brown & Co. Norfolk, Conn.	U.S. Norfolk	18,000
Norwich Arms Co. Norwich, Conn.	U.S. Norwich	25,000
Parkers', Snow & Co. Meriden, Conn.	U.S.-Parkers', Snow & Co. Meriden, Conn.	15,000
Providence Tool Co. Providence, R.I.	U.S.-Providence or U.S. Providence Tool Co. Providence, R.I.	70,000
E. Remington & Sons Ilion, New York	U.S.-Remington's Ilion, N.Y.	40,000
E. Robinson New York	U.S.-E.Robinson New York	30,000
Savage Revolving Fire Arms Co. Middletown, Conn.	U.S.-Savage R.F.A. Co. Middletown, CON.	25,250
C.D.Schubarth & Co. Providence, R.I.	U.S.- C.D. Schubarth Providence	9,500
S. Norris & W. T. Clement Springfield, Mass.	U.S.-S.N. & W.T.C. for Massachusetts	not known (several thousand)
J.T. Hodge & A.M. Burton Trenton, N.J.	U.S.-Trenton	11,495
Union Arms New York, N.Y.	U.S.-U.A.Co. New York	not known (several thousand)
Charles B. Hoard Watertown, N.Y.	U.S.-Watertown	12,800
Eli Whitney Whitneyville, Conn.	E. Whitney New Haven or Whitneyville	14,000
Dinslow & Chase Windsor Locks, Conn.	U.S.-Windsor Locks	not known (very few)

Once in the field, Ordnance officers looked on all of these arms as identical and issued them without regard to manufacturers. A typical volunteer company, Co. H, 11th Illinois Infantry listed the following in their possession in 1863.

Amoskeag Manf. Co. Manchester, N.H.	— 13
Wm. Muir & Co. Windsor Lock Co. Conn.	— 17
U.S. Manf. Co. Norwich	— 9
Wm. Mason Taunton, Mass.	— 4
Parker Snow & Co. Meridan, Conn.	— 4
Providence Tool Co. Providence, R.I.	— 4
U.S. Springfield Manf. Springfield	— 5
Total	56

Special Model 1861 and Model 1863 Rifle Muskets

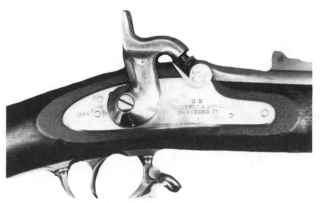

Special Model 1861 by Colt.

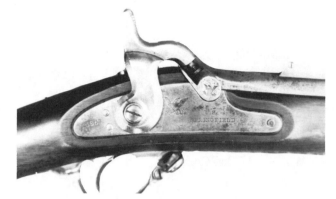

M1863 rifle musket.

Specifications

Length: 56''

Weight: about 9 lbs.

Caliber: .58

Bayonet: angular

The special model 1861 and the 1863 rifle muskets were similar in appearance to the model 1861 and identical in function. There were several differences, however, which make them a distinct and separate arm.

The special model 1861 was a contract-produced weapon. The model 1863 was produced by the U.S. Government Armory at Springfield, Massachusetts and by a single contractor. There were three deviations from the standard model 1861 which were evident on both these arms. First was the elimination of a small clean-out screw in the bolster immediately below the nipple. Next was the use of screw-tightened, clamp type barrel bands. Finally was the elimination of band retaining springs which on the model 1861 were seen in the stock just ahead of each barrel band.

In addition to these changes the special model 1861 had a slightly redesigned lock plate. A later version of the model 1863 reintroduced the band retaining springs when it was found that the band screws worked loose during firing.

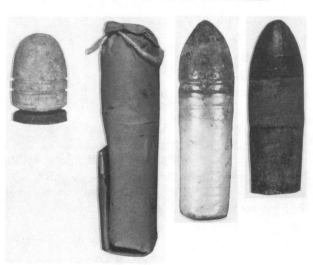

Patented ammunition for .58 cal. rifle muskets: Williams Type III (left), Johnston & Dow (center), and Bartholow (right).

18

British Pattern '53 "Enfield Rifle Musket"

Specifications

Length: 55.3''

Weight: about 9 lbs.

Caliber: .577

Bayonet: angular

The British pattern 1853 rifle musket bears the distinction of being the second most widely used infantry weapon in the Civil War. The arm was imported in large quantities by both the North and the South and saw service in every major battle from Shiloh in April 1862 to the final engagements of 1865.

The pattern '53 was the standard arm of the British army from 1853 to 1867. Originally produced for British service at the Royal Small Arms Factory at Enfield, England, the "Enfield" was both well made and deadly accurate.. An important consideration from an American standpoint was its .577 caliber that allowed the use of the same ammunition made for the .58 caliber arms which were standard in both the United States and Confederate armies.

It is estimated that 900,000 pattern '53 Enfields were brought to this continent during the years 1861 through 1865. Most of these were expressly made for the American market by independent contractors in London or Birmingham, England. Many still will be found with the maker's name, such as "Ward & Sons Makers, Birm." stamped in the stock near the butt plate. Few, if any of those imported were actually made at Enfield.

English-made cartridge and bullet, and C.S.-made bullet (right). Federals used standard .58 cal. cartridges.

19

C.S. Richmond Rifle and Rifle Musket

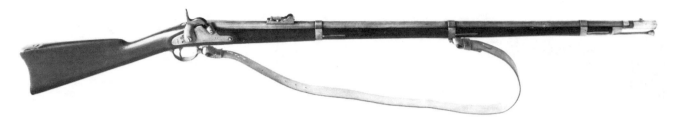

Specifications

Length: 56"

Weight: about 9 lbs.

Caliber: .58

Bayonet: angular

The C.S. Richmonds were often referred to as "Confederate Springfields" a term which attests not only to their appearance but to their quality as well, All of these weapons saw Confederate service.

C.S.-made cartridges for .577/.58 cal. weapons: Gardner patent (left), Columbus, GA (center), and Lynchburg (right).

The C.S. Richmond rifles and rifle muskets were produced in larger quantity that any other Confederate made firearms. These well-made arms were close copies of the U.S. M1855 rifle and M1855/61 rifle musket. They were, in fact, made on the exact same machinery.

When the Harpers Ferry Armory and Arsenal was captured by Virginia state troops in April 1861, the machinery from that extensive facility was moved to Richmond, Virginia. This machinery, which represented nearly half of the U.S. government arms producing capability, became the backbone of Confederate small arms production. That part of the machinery which remained in Richmond continued to be used for arms manufacture until the fall of Richmond in 1865.

There are several distinct differences in the Richmond-produced arms when compared to their Yankee counterparts. The most noticeable is the plain "hump-back" lock plate. To facilitate manufacture, the Confederates immediately eliminated the Maynard tape priming system found on the M1855 Harpers Ferry arms. Because they continued to use the Harpers Ferry dies, the resulting lock retained the outline of the M1855. This distinctive lock was then stamped "C.S." over "Richmond, Va." forward of the hammer with the date of manufacture to the rear.

Additional differences were also made to ease manufacture. These included the substitution of a brass butt plate and nose cap for the harder to produce, iron parts found on Harpers Ferry arms. Another economy measure was the total elimination of the model 1855 iron patch box.

Austrian "Lorenz" Rifle Musket

Specifications

Length: 52.75''

Weight: about 8 lbs.

Caliber: .54 - .59

Bayonet: angular

Although several types of muskets were imported from Austria, the model 1854 rifle musket, known as the "Lorenz," was the most widely used. Second only in imports to the British pattern '53 Enfield, the Lorenz saw service in both theaters of the war. The Lorenz was imported in several calibers, but the most popular and most commonly used was the .54 caliber.

Evidence has shown a heavy concentration of Lorenz rifle muskets in the Confederate Army of Tennessee and other Confederate units in the western theater, with significant numbers being issued in 1863 and 1864. Like the Enfield, importing of Austrian arms began in the later part of 1861, by the North and South. Also like its British counterpart, the Lorenz rifle musket continued to arrive in large numbers throughout the war.

"New Model" bullet (left) imported by C.S. and U.S.-made bullet and cartridge (center and right).

21

Belgian and French Muskets, Rifles and Rifled Muskets

Specifications

Length: 56"

Weight: about 9 lbs.

Caliber: .69

Bayonet: angular

The numerous models of small arms imported from Belgium and France are often similar in appearance, but vary greatly in quality. Prior to the war, the extensive Belgian arms producing facilities located in Liege made numerous small arms for export. Many of the arms were based on earlier French designs. During the same period the French military was experimenting with a number of different weapons designs. These factors combined to make available for sale a substantial number of small arms of assorted patterns. The United States and the Confederacy proved a most willing market. When issued by Union or Confederate ordnance officers, these arms were often lumped together in categories such as "Rifled Muskets, Belgian or French, brass or bright-mounted. Calibre .69."

The French model 1859 rifle was one of the best of the imported arms. It was manufactured in both Belgium and France in .577 caliber, and was considered a first class arm by the U.S. Ordnance Department. The gun was well liked by those who carried it. On the other hand, most of the "Belgian or French" rifled muskets with calibers ranging from .69 to .71 were considered worthless by those who were forced to use them. The 102nd Pennsylvania was issued such an arm in 1861. The regiment was engaged in action during the Peninsula campaign in May 1862 and after the battles of Williamsburg and Fair Oaks, the "Belgium" muskets had disappeared. In their place were Springfields and Enfields "requisitioned" from the two battlefields.

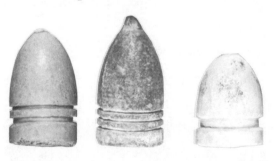

Confederate-made and used bullets for .69 cal. rifled muskets: Gardner patent (left), Belgian (center), and French "triangular" cavity (right).

Saxon Rifle Muskets Model 1851 and 1857, "The Dresden Rifle Musket"

Specifications

Length: 53"

Weight: about 9 lbs.

Caliber: .58

Bayonet: angular

The Saxon rifle muskets models of 1851 and 1857 were among the best made of the many foreign import arms. They were purchased in Dresden, Germany and were often referred to as the "Dresden rifle" by the men who carried them.

Some 27,000 of the model 1851 and 1857 were imported to the United States early in the war. The only difference between the two models was the barrel length; model 1857 being three inches longer than the earlier model. The fact that nearly all of these were issued is attested to by the numerous photographs which exist today of Union soldiers proudly holding them. The most distinctive feature of these weapons was the unique double middle barrel band.

During the war, the U.S. Ordnance Department considered the "Dresden" a first class arm, a fact which speaks well for its construction and reliability.

U.S. produced Williams "regulation" ammunition for .577/.58 cal. weapons.

RIFLES

Model 1841 "Mississippi" Rifle

Model 1841 "Palmetto" Rifle

Fayetteville Rifle

Whitworth Rifle

"American" Rifle

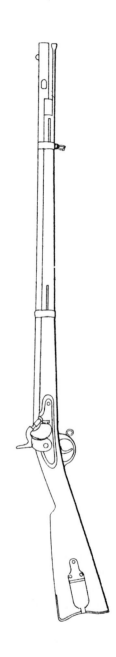

Model 1841 Rifle, "The Mississippi Rifle"

Specifications

Length: 48.75''

Weight: about 9¾ lbs.

Caliber: .54 & .58

Bayonet: sword or angular

The U.S. model 1841 rifle was one of the most famous and widely used arms of its type. The model 1841 first gained recognition in the hands of a regiment of Mississippi volunteers in the Mexican War, hence the nickname "Mississippi."

An exceptionally handsome rifle, the model 1841 was fitted with brass barrel bands and trigger guard. Added to this was a large brass patch box set in its dark walnut stock. Originally issued in .54 caliber, many model 1841's were rerifled to the standard U.S. government .58 caliber after 1855. In either caliber, the "Mississippi" was well known for its deadly long range accuracy.

The model 1841 was produced at the U.S. Armory at Harpers Ferry, Virginia and by four contractors. Production of this arm began in 1842 and continued until 1855. During this period over 75,000 model 1841 rifles were manufactured. At the outbreak of the war, the State of New York purchased 5,000 model 1841 rifles from Remington Arms of Herkimer County, N.Y.

The model 1841 saw extensive service in the hands of soldiers from both the Union and Confederacy. It was a favorite arm of Confederate mounted troops as well as the infantry on both sides. One of the Union regiments engaged at Gettysburg on July 1, 1863, the 45th New York Infantry, was armed with this rifle.

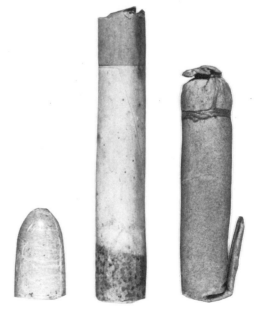

C.S. Macon Arsenal bullet and cartridge (left) for the "Mississippi," and earlier round shot cartridge (right). Federals used standard .54 cal. ammunition (see Austrian).

Model 1841 "Palmetto" Rifle

Specifications

Length: 49"

Weight: about 9¾ lbs.

Caliber: .54

Bayonet: none

The model 1841 "Palmetto" rifle was manufactured in 1852-1853 by Wm. Glaze & Co. in Columbia, South Carolina. Only about 1,000 of these rifles were made. They were an exact duplication of the U.S. model 1841 "Mississippi" rifle.

The Wm. Glaze contract was with and for the State of South Carolina and these arms were used to arm the militia of that state. Even though they predated the Civil War by nine years, these rifles were certainly all used in the war by South Carolina volunteers. The quality and workmanship was equal to any of the northern made M1841's. The lock plate was marked with a palmetto tree encircled by the words "Palmetto Armory, S.C." forward of the hammer. To the rear of the hammer was stamped "Columbia, S.C. 1852."

Confederate Gardner patent ammunition for .54 cal. muzzleloading weapons.

26

Fayetteville Rifle

Specifications

Length: 49''

Weight: about 8½ lbs.

Caliber: .58

Bayonet: sword

The Fayetteville rifle was produced in Fayetteville, North Carolina, using machinery which had been captured at the U.S. Armory at Harpers Ferry, Virginia, in April 1861. The site of manufacture was the former U.S. arsenal which had been seized by the state of North Carolina in April 1861 as well.

Production began at Fayetteville in the spring of 1862 and continued until March 1865. Fayetteville rifles resemble the U.S. model 1855 rifle including the barrel lug for the M1855 sword bayonet. A copy of this bayonet was also manufactured at Fayetteville.

As with most Confederate made copies of U.S. arms there were deviations incorporated to ease manufacture. The butt plate and nose cap on the Fayetteville rifles were of brass rather than iron. Also present on early production Fayettevilles is the plain "hump-back" lock plate seen on C.S. Richmond arms. This was a result of using blank locks captured from Harpers Ferry which had not been milled for the Maynard tape primer found on M1855 U.S. arms. The lock is stamped "Fayetteville" forward of the hammer with an eagle over "C.S.A." The date of manufacture appears back of the hammer.

Fayetteville rifles were a fine example of the Confederate ability to adapt and meet the needs of the new nation. The arms were well made and rivaled U.S. produced arms in quality, if not quantity. Many Fayetteville arms were used in the eastern Confederate armies, but some were undoubtedly supplied to those operating west of the mountains.

Full package of Confederate cartridges (with x-ray) made for .577/.58 cal. rifled arms.

Sharpshooter Rifles

Sharpshooter (sniper) rifles can be loosely defined as those intended for accurate shooting at very long ranges. During the Civil War these varied from carefully made, high grade military arms, such as the British Whitworth, to individually handcrafted American made target rifles. These weapons were often outfitted with precision telescopic sights. Despite their diversity in caliber, weight and dimensions, they all had one thing in common: in the hands of skilled marksmen, they were deadly.

British Whitworth Rifle

The British Whitworth looked very much like the pattern '53 Enfield rifle musket. It was here, however, that the similarity ended. The Whitworth was a .45 caliber arm with a hexagonal bore. The unique Whitworth bullet was shaped to fit the bore. Also unique was the mounting position of the telescopic sight. When so outfitted this sight was mounted on the left side of the stock opposite the lockplate. With a telescopic sight this rifle could be counted on for killing accuracy at ranges up to 1500 yards.

Most Whitworths which entered this country during the war did so through Southern ports and it was a favorite arm of Confederate sharpshooters. Despite the limited number of Whitworths imported, the rifle saw service in both eastern and western theaters throughout the war.

Specifications

Length: 48.75''

Weight: almost 10 lbs.

Caliber: .45

Bayonet: none

English-made patented "tube" cartridges: cylindrical (left) and hexagonal (right).

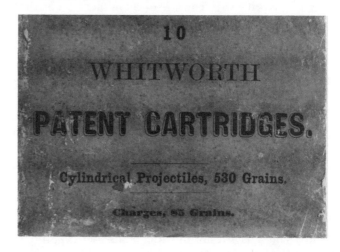

Specifications

Length: varies considerably

Weight: 12 - 35 lbs.

Caliber .36 - .50

Bayonet: none

The "American Rifle"

The "American Rifle," as individually crafted target rifles were known, were precision instruments. These rifles were always fitted with either telescopic or finely adjusted peep sights. Because they were individually made, physical appearance and dimensions varied greatly. The weight of these arms ranged from about 9 pounds to nearly 35 pounds. Those of the heaviest weight, over 12 or 13 pounds, were intended to be fired from a rest. Near pinpoint accuracy at ranges to 1,000 yards could be expected of these rifles. A target the size of an enemy soldier was an easy mark at much greater distances.

Several companies and three full regiments of men were raised to serve as sharpshooters in the Union army. Most Confederates so employed did so within the ranks of normal infantry regiments. During the final year of the war, battalions of sharpshooters were formed within both the Union and Confederate armies. These battalions consisted of the best marksmen from each of the infantry regiments serving with the command. The business of killing had taken a professional turn.

"Picket" bullets for target and other rifles, in assorted calibers.

29

BREECHLOADING RIFLES

Colt Revolving Rifle

Henry Rifle

Merrill Rifle

Sharps Rifle

Spencer Rifle

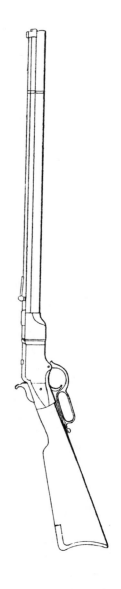

Colt Revolving Rifle

Specifications

Length: 50''

Weight: almost 10 lbs.

Caliber: .56

Bayonet: sword or angular

This unique rifle was first produced in 1855 and was submitted to the U.S. army for field tests in 1857. As its name would suggest, it was produced by Colt Firearms Mfg. Company and was designed as a greatly enlarged version of the famous Colt revolver. Despite the success of the revolver, the revolving rifle was considered too complex for military use. This belief was overshadowed by the war emergency and some 4,600 were purchased by the government for issue to volunteers.

The first real combat use of the Colt revolving rifle was in the hands of the 1st and 2nd United States Sharpshooters. These men had grudgingly accepted the rifles and used them during the early Spring of 1862 until they were rearmed with the Sharps rifles they had originally been promised. In contrast, the 21st Ohio Infantry received and used the Colt revolving rifle for its entire term of service. Well-liked, but considered too long for use on horses, the 2nd Michigan Cavalry used them until March 1864. The 21st Ohio made telling use of their Colts during the battle of Chickamauga when they assisted the Spencer rifle-armed "Lightning Brigade" in the heroic rear guard defense on Snodgrass Hill. When the war ended, the few Colt revolving rifles remaining in service were sold as surplus by the U.S. government for as little as 40 cents each.

Henry Rifle

Specifications

Length: 43.5''

Weight: 9¼ lbs.

Caliber: .44

The Henry rifle stands alone as the most technically advanced firearm to see service during the Civil War. The Henry was a lever action magazine fed arm, and its fire power was unequaled. Although only 1,731 Henry rifles were purchased by the Federal government, many more saw service in the hands of soldiers who were willing to pay the $40.00 necessary to privately purchase them.

In the days when muzzle-loading rifles were by far the most widely used weapons and when single shot breech-loaders were considered advancements, the Henry's 15 shot magazine (located under the barrel) offered a decided advantage. Students of arms who are familiar with the famed Winchester lever action rifle (still in common use today) can immediately see its similarity to the Henry. This is more than coincidental. Although the patent for the arm was held by its inventor, B. Tyler Henry, his employer, Oliver F. Winchester, held the rights to the patent.

It was Winchester who first tried to convince the Federal government to purchase this revolutionary new weapon in the early days of the war. The Chief of Ordnance, Brigadier General James W. Ripley, recommended that the rifle not be purchased, disliking the weight of the arm when loaded and seeing no advantage over single shot breech-loading arms. Also, the special copper-cased cartridge, a .44 caliber rimfire, was not usable in any other arm.

The only arms which came close to the Henry in technology were the Spencer rifle and carbine. The Spencer had the distinct advantage of being easier to produce; this was a major factor in the Spencer becoming the dominant magazine fed arm of the war.

Despite government reluctance and Spencer competition, by 1865 over 10,000 Henry rifles had been produced, many of which saw service in the war.

Merrill Rifle

Specifications

Length: 48.5''

Weight: about 9 lbs.

Caliber: .54

Bayonet: sword

The Merrill Rifle is one of the numerous breech-loading systems that flourished largely due to the war emergency. The Merrill employed a unique top opening loading mechanism, the shooter had to raise the lever back towards himself, thus exposing a chamber into which he inserted the bullet with its combustible cartridge. When the chamber lever was closed, a small piston which was connected to it and which rode in a track back of the cartridge chamber, forced the cartridge itself forward and seated it and the bullet in the chamber. Its paper cartridge employed an external priming system. In this case, it took the form of a standard musket cap which was ignited by a lock and hammer identical to a standard musket's.

Only 769 Merrill rifles were purchased for issue by the Federal government. Despite this small number, the arms saw use in both theaters of the war. In the East, part of the 1st Battalion Massachusetts Sharpshooters were armed with Merrills, who served with distinction at Gettysburg as part of the Union 2nd Corps and assisted in the repulse of Pickett's Charge. In the Western theater, the 21st Indiana Infantry (which later became the 1st Indiana Heavy Artillery) also used the Merrill rifle. Both regiments spoke highly of the Merrill's accuracy.

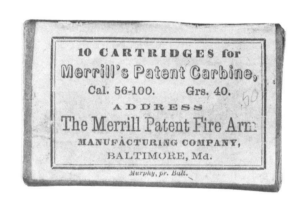

Sharps Rifle

Specifications

Length: 47''

Weight: 8¾ lbs.

Caliber: .52

Bayonet: angular or sword

The Sharps rifle is the best known of several breech-loading rifles used during the war. This fame is largely due to the rifle's use by the legendary 1st and 2nd regiments of the United States Sharpshooters. The Sharps is a breech-loading single shot rifle. It was necessary for its user to open the breech and manually insert a cartridge each time he wished to fire. Although this method of loading did not equal the rate of fire of such arms as the Spencer and Henry rifles, it was a significant improvement over the muzzle-loading arms in general use during the war. Breech-loading allowed the user to load and fire with ease while he was laying down or was otherwise concealed from enemy fire. Thus, it was ideally suited to non-conventional uses, such as sharpshooting.

The Sharps used a totally combustible cartridge made of linen or nitrate treated paper. The cartridge was totally consumed by the ignition of the powder charge it contained when the rifle was fired. The cartridge was externally primed, thus it was necessary for the soldier to place a standard musket percussion cap on a nipple found on the rifle's breech which was struck by the rifle's hammer to achieve ignition.

Spencer Rifle

Specifications

Length: 47''

Weight: 10 lbs.

Caliber: .52

Bayonet: angular

The Spencer rifle shares the spotlight with the Henry as the most technically advanced and effective small arm of the war. Invented by Christopher Spencer, a young Connecticut-born former Colt Firearms employee, the Spencer was an idea whose time had come. Because it took time to sell anyone in the U.S. army or navy on his new concept in firearms design, it was not until January 1863 that the first Spencer rifles were available and issued for field use. From that time on, however, the fire power of the Spencer wrote its own chapter in the history of warfare. This chapter foretold things to come in wars of the future.

Christopher Spencer's rifle featured a tubular feed magazine which held seven internally primed, metallic case .56 caliber cartridges. This magazine was contained in the rifle's butt stock and was itself loaded through the butt plate. By means of lever action, the rifle's ingenious mechanism first ejected an empty cartridge case from a previously fired round and then fed a fresh cartridge into the chamber. The soldier had then to only cock the external hammer, aim, and shoot. The Spencer's rate of fire was limited only by the user's speed in firing.

The first to be armed with the Spencer rifle were the 5th, 6th, 7th, and 8th Independent Companies of Ohio Sharpshooters. The first Cavalry regiments were the 5th and a few of the 6th Michigan. The latter two regiments served with Custer's Brigade at Gettysburg.

The first real combat test of the Spencer was the Battle of Hoover's Gap, Tennessee, on June 24, 1863. In this battle, a brigade of Union mounted infantry, consisting of the 17th and 72nd Indiana and the 92nd, 98th, and 123rd Illinois under the command of Colonel John T. Wilder, decimated a numerically superior Confederate infantry force. On this day, Wilder's Brigade earned the nickname "The Lightning Bri-

gade." Armed with their Spencer rifles, the Brigade continued to live up to this name throughout the bloody campaigns of the Western theater of the War.

CARBINES

Ballard Carbine

Burnside Carbine

Cosmopolitan Carbine

Gallager Carbine

Gibbs Carbine

Model 1843 Hall Carbine

Maynard Carbine

Merrill Carbine

Sharps Carbine and C.S. Sharps

Smith Carbine

Spencer Carbine

Starr Carbine

Model 1855 Pistol Carbine

Double-barrel Shotgun

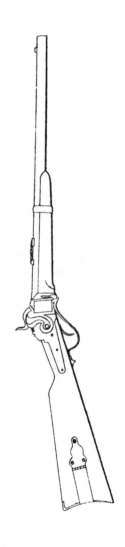

Ballard Carbine

Specifications

Length: 38''

Weight: 7 lbs.

Caliber: .44

The Ballard carbine was one of the better small arm designs introduced during the war. This arm was a single shot breech-loader employing internally primed metallic cartridges. The Ballard design conquered one of the greatest failings of other metallic cartridge arms; the ejection of the fired cartridge casing. This was done by means of a manually operated, spring-loaded ejecting rod located under the breech. Once the breech was opened, the simple rearward pull of a small knob protruding through the fore-stock moved the rod and kicked out the casing.

The operating mechanism of the Ballard consisted of a dropping breech block which contained both the hammer and trigger. A downward motion of the operating lever/trigger guard lowered the block and exposed the breech. The reverse motion both closed the breech and placed the hammer on half-cock.

Despite the well made and effective design of the Ballard, only 1,509 were purchased by the Federal government. This was offset, however, by the purchase of nearly 20,000 by the State of Kentucky for issue to troops from that state.

Burnside Carbine

Specifications

Length: 39.5''

Weight: about 7 lbs.

Caliber: .54

The Burnside carbine was the third most widely used carbine in the Union cavalry. Beginning in 1861, and continuing throughout the war, the U.S. government purchased and issued over 50,000 Burnside carbines. This number was exceeded only by the Spencer and Sharps carbines.

The breech-loading mechanism of the Burnside was simple and effective. By lowering the operating lever, which also served as a trigger guard, a rectangular steel block contained in the breech was tilted up. This block contained a cone shaped cavity into which the metallic cartridge of the same shape was dropped with the bullet end facing up. By closing the lever, the block rotated forward, fitting the bullet into the chamber. Ignition was by means of a standard musket cap exploded by an external hammer. A small hole in the base of the cartridge allowed the fire to pass through.

Despite the large number of Burnside carbines issued, the arm was disliked by many of its recipients. One complaint which was prevelant was the weakness of the spring holding the lever shut. A second, more serious objection, was the tendency of the cartridge casing to stick in the breech block after firing.

The Burnside saw extensive use in both theaters of the war. Captured Burnsides were widely used by Confederate cavalry. Toward the end of the conflict, the Burnside Rifle Co. received a contract to switch to the production of Spencer carbines. The age of the externally primed cartridge was drawing to a close.

Cosmopolitan Carbine

Specifications

Length: 39"

Weight: about 6½ lbs.

Caliber: .52

The Cosmopolitan carbine has the distinction of being the only such arm purchased by the Federal government, made west of the Alleghenies. It was manufactured by the Cosmopolitan Arms Company located in Hamilton, Butler County, Ohio.

The Cosmopolitan was very distinctive in appearance, with its long S-shaped external hammer, a scroll-like operating lever, and a barrel with no fore-stock. The carbine was operated by lowering the operating lever which in turn caused a steel block in the receiver to drop down, exposing the cartridge chamber. A cartridge was inserted and the lever closed. Ignition was by means of a standard percussion cap.

Over 9,000 Cosmopolitan carbines were purchased by the Federal government beginning in June 1862. Although many who were issued these carbines felt they were satisfactory, serious objections were raised by several regiments. The 8th Ohio Cavalry felt them to be "... an inefficient and unreliable weapon." Among their objections were: "The carbine does not carry to the sights (inaccurate). After a few discharges it leaks fire. The least jar will break some of its parts or the stock." These and other objections were sustained by the Chief Ordnance Officer of the Department of West Virginia in August 1864, who condemned the carbine as ".... a very worthless weapon .... thrust upon the Ordnance Department by political influence of contractors."

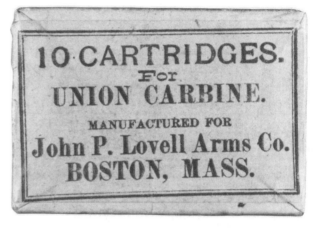

The Cosmopolitan carbine was known by several names, including Gwyn & Campbell, Union, Ohio, and "grapevine."

Gallager Carbine

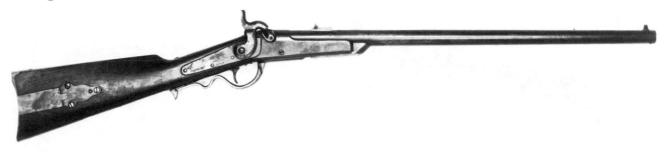

Specifications

Length: 39''

Weight: 7½ lbs.

Caliber: .50

The Gallager carbine was the invention of a southerner, Mahlon J. Gallager, of Savannah, Georgia. Despite its heritage, the arm itself was produced in Philadelphia, Pa., and is numbered among the various types issued to the Union cavalry.

The Gallager employed a breech-loading mechanism which consisted of a lever/trigger guard combination which, when pushed down, allowed the barrel to slide forward and tilt up and away from the breech. The brass case cartridge was then inserted directly into the breech end of the barrel itself. Raising the lever repositioned the barrel and seated the base of the cartridge into the breech. Ignition was obtained by a standard musket cap being exploded by an external hammer.

Nearly 18,000 Gallager carbines were issued during the war. The arm, however, was not well liked, due primarily to difficulty in removing the cartridge casing from the barrel after firing.

Gibbs Carbine

Specifications

Length: 39''

Weight: 7-3/8 lbs.

Caliber: .52

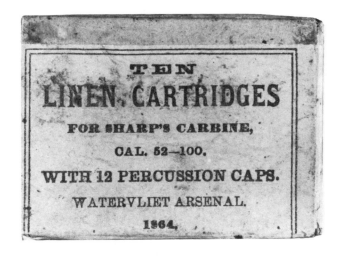

The Gibbs carbine saw only a very limited service in the war. Only 1,050 were purchased by the Federal government before a fire destroyed the factory. About half of this scant issue was sent to Missouri, the rest were issued to the Army of the Potomac.

The Gibbs mechanism was simple. An operating lever/trigger guard was lowered, which caused the barrel to slide forward a short distance and tip upward. The soldier inserted a linen cartridge into the barrel chamber. Reversing the motion closed the breech and seated the cartridge.

A Union ordnance officer reporting on the 300 Gibbs carbines in the Army of the Potomac in August 1863 made the following statement: "I cannot report favorably on the arm. The working is very simple but perfectly exposed rendering it liable to catch all dirt, and the smallest stick or pebble getting into it renders it unserviceable, until it is taken apart and cleaned."

The Gibbs carbine used Sharps ammunition - an early standardization attempt by the Federal government.

41

Hall Carbine Model 1843

Specifications

Length: 40''

Weight: 8¼ lbs.

Caliber: .52

The Hall carbine Model 1843 predated the Civil War by 18 years and was itself a modification of a design in use since 1833. The Hall employed a rising breech block which was activated by a lever located on the right side of the arm above the trigger. Pressure on the lever caused the carbine breech to tilt upward, allowing the soldier to place a paper cartridge into the breech. Repositioning the lever closed the breech and aligned the bullet with the barrel. Ignition was by means of a standard musket cap being struck by a hammer contained in the breech block.

The full use of the Hall carbine in the war is not fully appreciated by many historians. Within the Union cavalry, about 5,000 saw action in the western theater of the war. These were largely in the hands of Illinois and Missouri cavalrymen. In the East, however, the Hall saw service at least through 1863 in the hands of the cavalry of the Army of Northern Virginia. This use is documented by ordnance returns for several regiments, including the famed 1st Virginia cavalry. This was due to prewar purchase by the State of Virginia.

Maynard Carbine

Specifications

Length: 36.63''

Weight: 6 lbs.

Caliber: .50

The Maynard carbine was one of the most accurate breech-loading carbines produced during the war. Despite its small size and comparatively light weight, it was rugged and well made.

The loading mechanism of the Maynard employed an operating lever/trigger guard. When this was pivoted down, the barrel raised to allow the insertion of a special metallic cartridge with an extra wide base. Reversal of the loading procedure repositioned the barrel. The wide base of the cartridge acted as a seal to prevent loss of explosive force when the arm was fired. This extra wide base also made the fired cartridge easy to pull from the chamber, thereby negating a common complaint of many Civil War breech-loading carbines. Ignition of the cartridge was by means of a standard musket cap exploded by an exposed hammer which was contained in the breech. The fire from the discharge of the cap passed through a small hole in the center of the cartridge base.

Several models of the Maynard carbine were used in the war but all functioned basically the same way. The 1st model Maynard was manufactured before the war. This model had a target quality rear sight and 2,369 of them were purchased by the states of Georgia, Florida, and Mississippi. No Maynards were purchased by the Federal government until June 1864. These later Maynards had standard military sights, but saw limited service due to the late date of their purchase.

43

Merrill Carbine

Specifications

Length: 37.375"

Weight: 6½ lbs.

Caliber: .54

The Merrill carbine employed the same unique top opening loading mechanism as did the Merrill rifle. To load, the trooper raised a lever on top of the carbine breech which exposed the cartridge chamber. He then inserted a paper cartridge. Upon closing the lever, a small piston contained in a track behind the chamber pushed the cartridge forward and seated the bullet. The cartridge was fired by means of a standard musket cap ignited by an external hammer.

Although over 15,000 Merrill carbines were issued to the Union cavalry beginning in 1861, the arm was never popular. By mid-1863 those still in use were concentrated in the western theater of the war, with only a very few still in use by Army of the Potomac cavalrymen.

Early war issues of Merrill carbines had resulted in many being captured by Confederate cavalry. The use of the Merrill by Southern horsemen was common. Requisitions for Merrill ammunition were often found in ordnance returns of Army of Northern Virginia cavalry regiments.

C.S.- made bullet on right.

Sharps Carbine

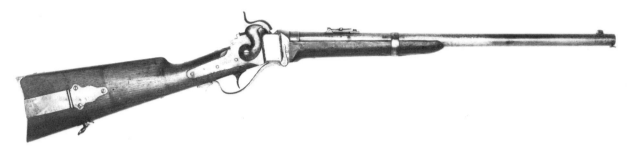

Specifications

Length: 39"

Weight: 7¾ lbs.

Caliber: .52

Sharps carbines were well known as a rugged and efficient arm for nearly the whole decade prior to the Civil War. The first Sharps used by U.S. forces were issued in 1854. From that time until the end of the Civil War it proved its value in every major cavalry action.

The Sharps carbine, like the Sharps rifle, used a paper or linen cartridge and fired a .52 caliber bullet. The Sharps carbines were also mechanically identical to the Sharps rifle. By means of a lever, which also served as a trigger guard, the soldier opened the carbine breech and loaded a single cartridge. The breech was closed and ignition was achieved by a standard musket cap which was exploded by an external hammer operated in the same way as a standard musket.

Both Union and Confederate cavalrymen liked the Sharps carbine and many favored it over other more advanced arms. As one Union ordnance officer reported, "A cavalry carbine should be very simple in its mechanism, with all its .... parts well covered from the splashing of mud, or the accumulation of rust and dust. Sharps carbine combines all these estimable qualities."

Specifications

Length: 39''

Weight: 7¾ lbs.

Caliber: .52

The simple mechanism of the Sharps carbine was copied by the Confederacy. This resulted in the manufacture first by the S.C. Robinson Co. of Richmond, Va. and later by the Confederate government, of some 5,000 Confederate Sharps carbines which were almost identical in appearance to their Northern counterparts. The failing of the Confederate Sharps came in the quality of manufacture, which resulted in a weapon prone to malfunctions in field use.

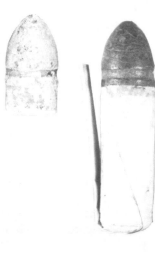

Smith Carbine

Specifications

Length: 39''

Weight: 7½ lbs.

Caliber: .50

The Smith carbine ranks fourth in the number of carbines purchased and issued by the Federal government. Over 31,000 Smiths were purchased for issue, beginning in January 1862.

The Smith carbine employed a unique and simple breech-loading system. By means of an upward pressure on a brass plunger located in front of the trigger, a spring steel strap on the top of the barrel was raised. This released the barrel, which then pivoted down and away from the breech. The cartridge was inserted into the chamber at the rear of the barrel. When the barrel was pivoted back into position, the base of the cartridge fit into the carbine breech. Ignition was achieved by a musket cap exploded by an external hammer.

The Smith was originally designed to use a cartridge with a hard rubber case. As with several other carbines, the greatest objection to the Smith was the difficulty often experienced in extracting the cartridge case after firing.

The use of Smiths early in the war resulted in many falling into the hands of Southern cavalrymen. For this reason, it is not uncommon to find requisitions for Smith ammunition in Confederate ordnance returns.

Thomas Poultney of Poultney & Trimble, Baltimore, MD was proprietor of Gilbert Smith's carbine invention when the Civil War began.

Spencer Carbine

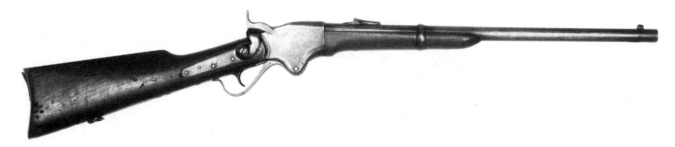

Specifications

Length: 39"

Weight: 8¼ lbs.

Caliber: .52

The Spencer carbine was not issued until October 1863. In spite of this late arrival, the Spencer proved to be the most popular and widely issued U.S. cavalry shoulder arm of the war. The Spencer carbine functions exactly the same as its predecessor, the Spencer rifle, and uses the same rim-fire metallic cartridge, but is 8 inches shorter. Both arms are lever action repeaters with a 7 round tubular magazine contained in the butt stock.

The development of the Spencer carbine was a direct result of reports such as the following, submitted by cavalry Ordnance Officer Capt. Wm. Redwood Price on Aug. 7, 1863: "The Spencer Repeating Rifle is used by the 5th and 6th Michigan Cavalry and is very highly spoken of by officers and men in those commands, as a rifle it is too heavy for the mounted service and is now used by those commands on foot mostly as skirmishers. I would recommend a similar arm with the barrel shortened to the size and weight of a carbine as the best arm for the cavalry service. A metallic cartridge is undoubtedly the best for cavalry, as a large amount of ammunition is wasted by jolting in the cartridge boxes, or becomes wet with rain or the fording of rivers. The Spencer cartridge contains within itself a perfect gas check and cap, and can be fired 8 times without taking it from the shoulder, one cartridge in the barrel and seven in the stock. The mechanism is very simple and tightly covered from dirt or rust. As a rifle it has had a thorough test in the field and is very popular."

In total, over 95,000 Spencer carbines were purchased by the Federal government. As with all other arms issued to the Union forces, some Spencers were captured and used by the Confederate army. The unique rim-fire cartridge of the Spencer proved too expensive and difficult for Confederate manufacturing facilities. The resulting necessity to rely solely on captured ammunition limited its use by Southern cavalrymen.

48

Starr Carbine

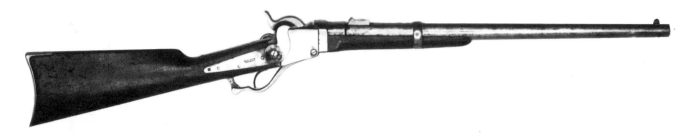

Specifications

Length: 37.625"

Weight: 7-3/8 lbs.

Caliber: .54

The Starr carbine was similar in appearance and function to the Sharps, but did not approach the quality of its famous look-alike. The Starr employed a dropping block action which was activated by the downward motion of the operating lever/trigger guard. This movement caused a block in the breech to drop below the rear of the barrel. The soldier then inserted a linen cased cartridge into the barrel chamber. The reverse movement of the lever closes the breech. Ignition was achieved by a musket cap and external hammer.

Despite the fact that over 20,000 Starr carbines were purchased during the war, the arm was not well liked. In August 1863, a Union ordnance officer reported his feelings as follows: "Starr's carbine . . . . is an evasion of Sharps patent with none of its virtues. The mechanism is too light and complicated, works well enough while perfectly new but the least dirt deranges it. It requires both hands to press back the lever, the cartridge is not readily placed straight in the barrel, and the gas check is very imperfect. After a few firings the salt petre corodes the barrel where it enters the gas check, rendering the lever doubly hard to open. As the part becomes more coroded, the effect of the discharge would be greatly impaired. When this occurs it could only be mended by a new barrel and new gas check, otherwise a new carbine."

49

Model 1855 Pistol-Carbine

Specifications

Length: 28.2''

Weight: about 5 lbs.

Caliber: .58

Bayonet: none

The model 1855 pistol-carbine was a single shot, muzzleloading percussion handgun which was equipped with a separate shoulder stock. The stock, when attached by the soldier to the handgrip of the pistol, effectively converted the pistol to a carbine. By this means the arm could be fired from the shoulder, increasing its stability and accuracy. The pistol-carbine fired virtually the same ammunition as the 1855 rifle musket. Like the rifle musket, it achieved ignition by the new Maynard tape primer. A total 4,021 of these arms were produced by the Springfield Armory in 1855 and 1856.

The pistol-carbine was a well made weapon, but it had one serious flaw. It was obsolete from the time of its first production. The six-shot revolver manufactured by Colt Firearms spelled the doom of the single-shot pistol.

Most of the pistol-carbines were still in various arsenals in 1861. The arms shortage brought on by the war meant actual combat use of this weapon. An unknown quantity, but probably most of those manufactured, were used to arm early volunteers.

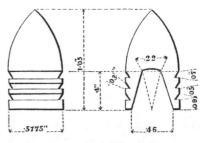

The 450-grain bullet adopted in 1855 for the new pistol-carbine.

Double-barrel Shotgun

Specifications

Length: varies greatly

Weight: varies greatly

Caliber: 12 gauge (.69)

Bayonet: none

If any firearm was in abundance in the South prior to the war, it was the double-barrel shotgun. Long a standby for hunting, nearly every family had, or had access to, such an arm. Due to its short effective range, the shotgun had limited value as an infantry weapon. It was in the close, sometimes hand-to-hand fighting common to mounted troops that the shotgun found a home.

Within the ranks of the Confederate cavalry the double-barrel shotgun was a favorite weapon. With its barrels shortened for ease in carrying on horseback, the resulting wide spread of the buckshot made the shotgun formidable and deadly in close combat.

By 1863, long-range, lever action, repeating carbines had become the ultimate cavalry weapon. In spite of this, many Confederate cavalrymen continued to rely on the double-barrel shotgun. Its twin charges of death-dealing buckshot served them well until the final days of the war.

REVOLVERS

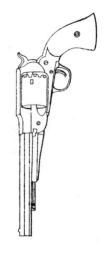

Adams Revolver

Model 1860 Colt ''Army'' Revolver

Model 1851 Colt ''Navy'' Revolver

Confederate ''Colt'' Revolvers

Kerr Revolver

Lefaucheux Revolver

LeMat Revolver

Model 1861 Remington ''Army'' Revolver

Model 1861 Remington ''Navy'' Revolver

Savage ''Navy'' Revolver

Spiller and Burr Revolver

Starr ''Army'' Revolver

Whitney ''Navy'' Revolver

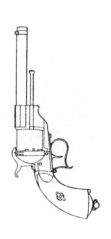

Adams Revolver

Specifications

Length: 11.5''

Weight: 2 lbs., 9 oz.

Caliber: .36

The Adams revolver had the unique distinction of being a British patent arm that was also manufactured in the United States. In England, Adams revolvers were produced by the London Armoury Company. In this country, the Massachusetts Arms Company of Chicopee Falls, Massachusetts was the manufacturer.

Prior to the war, about 600 Adams revolvers were purchased on a trial basis by the United States Army, but the arm was not adopted. Numerous other Adams revolvers were brought into this country by commercial firearms dealers. These pistols were privately purchased and were carried by a few officers and enlisted men in both the Union and Confederate armies. The Adams was a double-action, five-shot percussion revolver of very high quality.

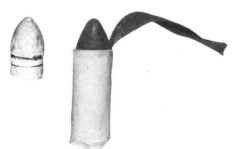

English-made bullet and cartridge.

53

Colt Revolvers Model 1860 Army and Model 1851 Navy

Specifications

"Army"

Length: 14"

Weight: 2 lbs., 11 oz.

Caliber: .44

Colt revolvers in calibers .44 and .36 were the most famous and widely used handguns to see service during the Civil War. These arms had gained reputations as effective and reliable weapons well before 1861.

The prominence of Colt revolvers in the years prior to the war meant that many could be found in private homes. Most of those in southern hands were carried to war by Confederate volunteers. Those in northern homes often went into service as the personal side-arms of Union officers.

Federal government purchases of Colt "Army" and "Navy" revolvers amounted to 38% of the total revolvers acquired for war use. Most of these went to arm Union cavalrymen.

All Colt "Army" and "Navy" pistols used during the war were six-shot, single-action, percussion revolvers. Colts were present on every field of battle from 1861-65. They were prized and well liked by all whose lives often depended upon them.

Ammunition for the Colt "Army" by Colt (left), Hazard (left center), D.C. Sage (right center), and Watervliet Arsenal (right).

Specifications

"Navy"

Length: 13"

Weight: 2 lbs., 10 oz.

Caliber: .36

Ammunition for the Colt "Navy" by Colt (left), Hazard (center), and an unidentified U.S. arsenal (right).

Confederate "Colt" Revolvers

Griswold & Gunnison.

Specifications

Griswold & Gunnison	*Leech & Rigdon*	*Dance Bros.*
Length: 13.25"	Length: 13"	Length: 11.5 & 13.5
Caliber: .36	Caliber: .36	Caliber: .36 & .44

Confederate copies of pre-war Colt revolvers are among the most interesting and rarest Civil War pistols. There were no less than seven different arms makers who produced these much needed side-arms for the South. Like the Confederacy itself, none of the southern companies producing Colt copies lasted more than a few years. The combined total output of all these firms was less than 7,000 arms. Most of these were look alike copies of the .44 caliber Colt "Dragoon" that had been produced in the 1850s. A few were a close duplication of the .36 caliber 1851 Colt "Navy." Like their northern counterparts, all were six-shot, single-action, percussion revolvers.

The very existence of these weapons spoke well for the popularity of Colt revolvers in the pre-war south. It also spoke well for the determination of the Confederate government to provide her sons with the best available arms.

All Confederate Colts were reliable, well made arms. None, however, achieved the fine quality and finish of the original product produced by the well established Colt factory in Hartford, Connecticut.

The most widely produced Confederate Colts were the work of the firm of Griswold and Gunnison, located in Griswoldville, Georgia. These revolvers had a distinctive brass frame (body) mounted with a steel cylinder and barrel.

The following companies are known to have manufactured Colt style revolvers for the Confederacy.

Company	Approx. Number Produced
August Machine Works Augusta, Georgia	100
Columbus Fire Arms Manf. Co. Columbus, Georgia	100
J.H. Dance & Bros. Columbia, Texas	500 (or less)
Griswold and Gunnison Griswoldville, Georgia	3,700
Leech and Rigdon Columbus, Mississippi	1,500
Rigdon, Ansley & Co. Augusta. Georgia	1,000
Schneider and Glassick Memphis, Tennessee	50

Dance Bros. "Navy".

Rigdon, Ansley & Company.

Confederate soldiers armed with a Griswold (above) and possibly an Augusta Machine Works revolver (left).

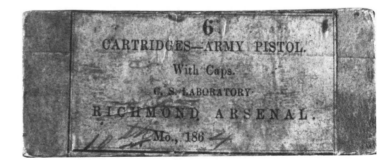

Colt "Navy" (left) and "Army" (right) ammunition made at the Richmond Laboratory.

Kerr Revolver

Specifications

Length: 10.8''

Weight: about 2½ lbs.

Caliber: .44

The Kerr revolver was one of the most interesting imported arms to see Civil War service. Kerr revolvers were manufactured by the London Armoury Company of London, England. Most, if not all, Kerr revolvers imported during the war years were purchased by the Confederate government, as shown in Confederate ammunition requisitions.

The Kerr could be fired either double or single-action. It was a five-shot, percussion revolver. There were without a doubt more Kerr revolvers carried by Confederate cavalrymen than all Confederate-made handguns combined. It was a well made, serviceable arm equal in quality to any revolver used in the war. The full story of Kerr revolvers has yet to be written.

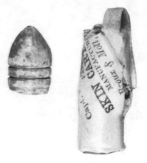

Lefaucheux Revolver

Specifications

Length: 11.5''

Weight: 2 lbs., 6 oz.

Caliber: 12mm (.44)

The French Lefaucheux revolver was one of the few foreign handguns imported by the United States government during the war. The substantial number purchased, nearly 12,000, rank it as one of the more significant handguns issued to Union troops. Most Lefaucheux's purchased by the North went to arm troops serving in the western theater.

The purchase of the Lefaucheux was at the same time important and remarkable. The importance lies in the fact that this was the only non-percussion revolver purchased for issue by either government. Equally important was that this was the first handgun issued to the U.S. Army that used internally primed ammunition. The Lefaucheux required a unique pin-fire cartridge which was difficult to manufacture and was used only by this arm.

Very few, if any, Lefaucheuxs were purchased by the Confederacy. It is well known, however, that some were carried by southern officers. No less a person than General T.J. "Stonewall" Jackson had an elaborately engraved Lefaucheux presented to him by his men.

LeMat Revolver

Specifications

Length: 14''

Weight: almost 4 lbs.

Caliber: .40 - revolver

16 gauge - shotgun

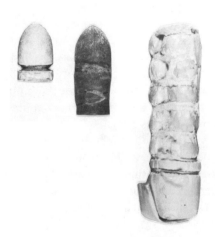

The LeMat revolver was the most exotic and formidable handgun to see service in the Civil War. The LeMat provided its user with a nine shot cylinder for .40 caliber pistol ammunition. This cylinder revolved around a separate .63 caliber smoothbore barrel which extended forward under the conventional .40 caliber rifled barrel. The smoothbore barrel was loaded with buckshot and fired separately. The LeMat was s single-action, percussion revolver. The hammer was fitted with a pivoting head which, when manually flipped down, redirected the strike to fire the shotgun barrel. For close combat the firepower of the LeMat was unequaled by any revolver of the time.

Although the LeMat was invented by a citizen of New Orleans, Louisiana it was produced in both Paris, France, and London, England. About 1,500 LeMat revolvers were imported by the Confederacy during the war. No purchases are known by the United States government.

The famous Confederate cavalry leader Gen. J.E.B. Stuart carried a LeMat revolver, as did several other Confederate generals.

Remington Revolvers Model 1861 Army and Model 1861 Navy

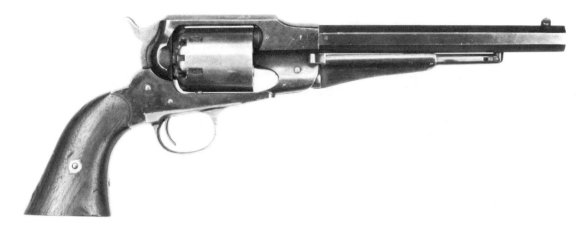

Specifications

"Army"	*"Navy"*
Length: 13.75"	Length: 13"
Weight: 2 lbs., 14 oz.	Weight: 2½ lbs.
Caliber: .44	Caliber: .36

Remington revolvers in .44 and .36 caliber were second only to Colts in the number that saw service during the Civil War. Remingtons accounted for nearly 35% of the revolvers purchased by the Federal government. Although the Remington Arms Company had been well established prior to the war, they had produced mostly long arms. For this reason, the number of Remington revolvers suitable for military use that were in private hands prior to 1861 was limited. With this in mind, it is clear why Remingtons were primarily a Union sidearm in the early war years. From 1863 on, Remingtons were also carried by many southern troopers, "donated" by some Union cavalrymen whose luck had run out.

Remington revolvers were six-shot, single-action, percussion arms. Because they lacked the pre-war reputation of Colts, they were never as popular in the minds of Civil War soldiers. Those who used them, however, found them a serviceable and reliable weapon.

Johnston & Dow's patent ammunition for Remington, Colt and other .36 and .44 cal. revolvers.

Savage Navy Revolver

Specifications

Length: 14.25''

Weight: 3 lbs., 7 oz.

Caliber: .36

The Savage "Navy" revolver was one of the most distinctive looking revolvers to see service in the war. Its appearance was dominated by an unusually large trigger guard containing two "triggers." One trigger terminated in a finger-sized ring. This was actually a lever which, when pulled, both rotated the cylinder and cocked the hammer.

About 12,000 Savage revolvers were purchased by the Federal government during the war. The majority of these were issued to cavalry in the western theater of the war. Many Savage revolvers were privately purchased and smuggled south. The arm was often seen in the hands of Confederate cavalry serving east of the Allegheny mountains.

The Savage "Navy" was a single-action, six-shot, percussion revolver. Because of its odd construction the arm was not well balanced and was therefore difficult to aim. A few Savage revolvers were purchased by Union officers, but they were was not a popular weapon.

Spiller and Burr Revolver

Specifications

Length: 12"

Caliber: .36

The Spiller and Burr revolver has the distinction of being the only Confederate-made handgun that was produced in quantity, but was not a Colt copy. Manufacturing difficulties had caused the makers to abandon the Colt design. Instead, they produced a cast brass frame .36 caliber revolver with a steel barrel and cylinder which followed the pattern of the all steel U.S. made Whitney "Navy" revolver.

The Spiller and Burr was first manufactured in Atlanta, Georgia. In January 1864 the firm was purchased by the Confederate government and the operation was moved to the Macon Armory in Macon, Georgia. The production of Spiller and Burrs continued in Macon until November 1864. Fearing capture of the valuable machinery by Union forces, the operation was moved to Columbia, South Carolina. The war ended, however, before production could resume. An estimated 1,400 Spiller and Burr revolvers were manufactured from June 1862 to November 1864.

Confederate-made cartridges for .36 cal. revolvers: Augusta (left) and Savannah (right).

Starr Army Revolvers

Specifications

	Single-action	Double-action
Length:	13.75''	11.625''
Weight:	3 lbs.	2 lbs., 12 oz.
Caliber:	.44	.44

The Starr "Army" revolvers were manufactured by Starr Arms Company of Yonkers, New York. They were the only American revolvers produced during the war that appeared in both single-action and double-action models.

The majority of Starr revolvers manufactured during the war were purchased by the U.S. government for issue to Union cavalry. This amounted to over 12% of the total revolvers acquired for issue.

As noted, the Starr could be found as either a single or double-action revolver. They were all six-shot, percussion arms. It is interesting to note that while the double-action Starr was the most modern by today's standards, more of the single-action models were actually made. The single-action was both cheaper to produce and more suited to the tastes of the time.

Whitney Navy Revolver

Specifications

Length: 13.125''

Weight: 2 lbs., 7 oz.

Caliber: .36

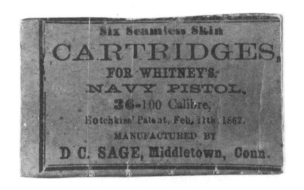

Over 30,000 Whitney "Navy" caliber revolvers were manufactured during the Civil War. Almost half of these were purchased by the U.S. government. These revolvers were nearly all issued to Union volunteer cavalry, with only a few actually seeing service in the U.S. Navy.

The Whitney "Navy" was manufactured by the Whitney Arms Company of New Haven, Connecticut. It was a six-shot, single-action, percussion revolver. Some Whitney "Navy" revolvers were purchased by the State of New Jersey and many were privately purchased by Union officers. The Whitney was a well made and very serviceable sidearm.

Accoutrements

The Civil War soldier was provided with a number of equipments for him to do his job. According to the U.S. 1861 *Ordnance Manual*, an infantryman's accoutrements are listed below:

CARTRIDGE BOX — made of black leather with two interior tins for holding forty cartridges.

CARTRIDGE BOX PLATE — a stamped brass oval embossed "US". Although decorative, the weight of this solder filled plate held the cartridge box flap down when it was unfastened.

CARTRIDGE BOX BELT — made of black leather it was attached to the cartridge box to provide a shoulder sling.

CARTRIDGE BOX BELT PLATE — a circular stamped brass decoration embossed with an "eagle" design. It, too, was solder filled.

CAP POUCH — made of black leather with an interior strip of sheep skin with the wool on. The pouch contained percussion caps and the *cone pick*.

BAYONET SCABBARD — made of black leather with a brass tip. Worn on the belt, this accoutrement transported the bayonet.

WAIST BELT — made of black leather for carrying the cap pouch and bayonet scabbard.

WAIST BELT PLATE — a stamped brass oval embossed "US", the hook arrangement embedded in the solder filling secured the ends of the waist belt.

GUN SLING — made of russet (brown) leather, it provided a means for carrying the infantry weapon, but was seldom used to steady the gun in aiming and firing.

Confederate regulations prescribed the same number of accoutrements; however, availability often limited the use of every item, especially the decorative cartridge box and cartridge box belt plates.

Among even the standard accoutrements, a large variety were produced in the North and South during the war. Some were intended for specific purposes such as cavalry carbine and revolver ammunition, while others were contractor variations.

Cartridge box with plate.

Cap pouch.

Waist belt plate.

Ammunition

Ammunition for Civil War small arms was more varied than the weapons themselves. As we shall see, the period of the early 1860s was one of great armament development - much of it brought on by the war itself with the need for serviceable arms. Weapon inventors and manufacturers (particularly of carbines and pistols) were inclined to make guns that required special, often patented, cartridges. These proprietary rounds were usually not made at the government arsenals and would therefore require the ordnance authorities to place orders for ammunition as well, if the arms were approved.

Coincidentally, it was also a time of great ammunition development (the Minie ball was less than ten years old). Patentees were constantly bombarding ordnance officers with new bullet and cartridge ideas for standard arms. Some of these inventions were worthless; however, others had merit and after testing were introduced into the ordnance pipelines.

A third reason for the great variety of ammunition was the fact that neither the North nor the South had a central laboratory or arsenal for fabricating small arms ammunition. Although the Confederacy made an effort with their facility at Macon, Georgia, the war did not last long enough for this to be fully accomplished. In the North, it does not appear that a central establishment was even considered. So even with strict regulations and guidelines, the sixteen Federal and Northern state arsenals (see Appendix A) and the eighteen smaller of Confederate arsenals and depots (see Appendix B) often made different cartridges and bullets for the same arms. In addition to this, the bullet and cartridge requirements were supplemented by purchases from private manufacturers and abroad.

The ammunition illustrated with the weapons on the following pages was employed by the particular arms; however, in many cases there were other types of cartridges used. It was not our intention in a study of this size to illustrate every cartridge used in every weapon.

Civil War small arms ammunition ran the gamut from simple to complex. Although it was possible to load most weapons with loose powder and ball, this was seldom necessary except in the case of some non-standard weapons that soldiers brought from home. Both the Union and Confederate ordnance departments were more than able to supply the needs of their troops in the field. Any spotty shortages were more logistical in nature than from manufacturing shortfalls.

The most common ammunition used with muzzleloaders during the war was the paper wrapped cartridge. Here, the bullet and powder charge were encased in paper, and it required that the soldier open the round to pour the powder down the barrel. Federal procedures demanded that the bullet be completely void of paper before it was rammed home; however, some Confederate and imported cartridges of this type were lubricated at the bullet end and were intended to be loaded still wrapped in the cartridge paper.

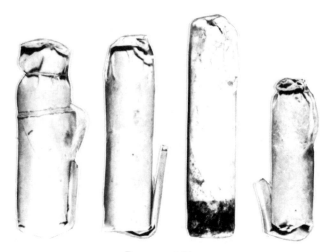

Paper cartridges.

Combustible cartridges fall into the category of separate primed ammunition that saw extensive use with carbines and revolvers. A combustible cartridge had the bullet attached to a cartridge case made of thin nitrated paper, linen, membrane, collodion or other substance that would be completely consumed by the powder charge explosion. It did not need to be opened to expose the powder, and was ignited by the flame from a regular percussion cap. Several combustible cartridges were adapted for use in muzzleloaders.

Other than the combustible cartridges, most separate primed cartridges were best suited for breechloading carbines and rifles, and were an important factor in sustaining an increased rate of fire. Generally, besides the combustible varieties, this type of cartridge had a case made of copper or brass, or brass and paper, or India rubber. The flame from the percussion cap penetrated through a small hole in the base of the case and ignited the powder charge.

Unfortunately, many of these "spent" cases were difficult to remove from the breech of the gun.

The most advanced types of ammunition used during the war were those that were internally primed, such as the rimfire, pin-fire, and certain evasions of Smith and Wesson's rimfire patent. The rimfire cartridge was completely self-contained: it had together in one piece the primer, powder, bullet, and case. The cartridge cases went through at least eight steps in the forming process before they were ready to be charged with fulminate, which was "spun" into the outer recesses of the "rim" at the base of the case. After the appropriate powder charge was inserted, the bullet was crimped into the open end of the case. In operation, the hammer of the gun struck the rim of the cartridge, igniting the fulminate and in turn the powder charge. An earlier development that saw limited use in this country was the pin-fire cartridge. Here, a stout, brass wire "pin" protruded through the side of the case. When struck by the hammer, the pin was driven into percussion compound that rested on an anvil. The resulting explosion ignited the powder charge.

Cartridges were packaged by the arsenals and manufacturers in many assorted ways. Generally, ammunition made at arsenals for muzzleloaders was put up in paper wrapped bundles of ten cartridges. Confederate wrappers are usually marked with the type of cartridge and place and date of manufacture. Regrettably, Union ammunition is not similarly identified, except on wooden packing crates for 1,000 rounds. Other methods of wrapping cartridges by private makers varied from pasteboard boxes to paper covered, drilled wooden blocks. The number of revolver cartridges in a package usually corresponded to the number of chambers in the weapon's cylinder.

One final observation of Civil War ammunition involves the actual diameter of bullets and the nominal caliber of weapons. Muzzleloaders had to use bullets that were smaller than the bore diameter, in order for the weapon to be loaded properly. Therefore, the .58 cal. M1861 Springfield rifle musket used a bullet .574 inches in diameter. Breechloading carbines and rifles, and revolvers used bullets larger than the bore diameter. Thus, the bullet for the .52 cal. Sharps carbine or rifle was actually .535 inches in diameter, and a .44 cal. Colt bullet was .455 inches in diameter. Packages and crates are sometimes marked with the bore diameter of the weapon and at other times with the diameter of the ammunition.

Combustible cartridges.

Separate primed cartridges.

Internally primed cartridges.

Appendages

Appendages, or "musket tools" as they are more commonly called today, were issued to soldiers so that they could maintain, clean and make minor field repairs to their weapons. Almost every gun had special tools that were designed just for it, the differences in weapon screw and nipple sizes, construction, and caliber made this necessary. The 1861 *Ordnance Manual* prescribed the following appendages for the M1855 arms:

WIPER — this tool was used to clean the bore of the gun. It was attached to the threaded end of the ramrod. The two pointed prongs held a piece of cloth that "wiped" the bore as the ramrod was moved in and out of the barrel. In an emergency, the wiper was often used as a ball-screw.

BALL-SCREW — often called a "worm" or "ball-puller" this tool was used to extract bullets from the bore when the charge failed to ignite or when the gun just needed to be unloaded. It too was attached to the threaded end of the ramrod. The screw-like projection was driven into the soft lead bullet and turned until it caught. When the ramrod assembly was withdrawn, the bullet was removed from the barrel.

SCREW-DRIVER — this tool performed a combination of disassembling chores. On one end was a cone or "nipple" wrench used to remove the nipple from the breech end of the barrel. Although the M1855 appendage had three screwdriver blades for the weapon's assorted-size screw slots, later U.S. regulation models had only two blades.

SPRING-VICE — in order to remove or replace the mainspring on the inside of the lock, the thumb-screw arrangement of this appendage was used to depress the spring in order to perform the operation.

BAND-SPRING and TUMBLER-PUNCH — another combination tool, this one was used to drive the pins of the barrel band-springs out of the forestock, and the tumbler from its tight fitting pivot in the lock.

TOMPION — inserted in the muzzle, this appendage was used daily to keep dirt and moisture from the weapon's bore. According to the 1861 *Ordnance Manual*, the M1855 tompion was made of maple wood, but others used a combination of materials like brass and wood; brass and cork; brass, rubber and felt; or rubber.

(Company records indicate that only non-commissioned officers carried or were issued the ball-screw, the spring-vice, and the band-spring and tumbler-punch.)

Other appendages:

CONE or "NIPPLE" PICK — carried in the cap

Wiper (left) and ball-screw (right).

Screw-driver (top) and spring-vice (bottom).

Band-spring and tumbler-punch (top) and tompions (bottom).

69

pouch, this thin wire tool was used to remove fouling, dirt or percussion cap debris from the cone.

CONE or "NIPPLE" PROTECTOR — only standard issue with P53 Enfields, this appendage protected the cone from damage and the elements. Many soldiers made their own cone protectors by carving lead bullets to the proper shape.

CARBINE BRUSH — this appendage was used in place of the wiper to clean the bores of breechloading carbines and rifles. A leather thong, attached to the end of the brass and bristle brush (some had thongs attached to both ends), was dropped through the barrel. The brush cleaned the bore as the thong was pulled.

Cone pick and cone protectors.

Carbine brush.

Assorted appendages or "musket tools."

70

Bayonets

Bayonets were detachable blades put on the muzzle ends of muskets and rifles, for use in hand-to-hand fighting. Most bayonets issued during the Civil War were one of two types: the angular (or socket) bayonet, or the sword (or saber) bayonet.

The three steel and/or iron parts of an angular bayonet were the blade, socket and clasp. The blade had a sharp point and usually three fluted sides (the Austrian quadrangular bayonet was a notable exception with four sides). The socket fit tightly over the outside of the muzzle and was secured to a stud on the barrel by the clasp. Generally, the front sight of the gun was used as the bayonet-stud for angular bayonets.

The sword bayonet looked like either a short saber or a large knife. It was made up of a pointed, steel blade, a brass hilt and a spring-clasp. The handle-like hilt included a muzzle-socket that fit over the end of the gun barrel. The spring-clasp secured the bayonet to a stud that was usually mounted on the side of the barrel. Sword bayonets were considered very unwieldy and were not popular with troops.

Most Civil War soldiers had heard or read tales of heroic bayonet charges that decided the outcome of many engagements during the Revolutionary and Mexican Wars. However, once in combat, men soon learned that the increased range and accuracy of rifled weapons made the bayonet charge almost obsolete. The number of soldiers on either side who received bayonet wounds was very small. Because of this, many bayonets were totally discarded or put to other uses: sword bayonets were used for cutting brush or butchering, and angular bayonets became tent pegs, pot hooks, candlesticks, skewers and intrenching tools.

Ignition

Ignition, in reference to small arms, is the method or means used to explode the powder charge. Under several specific weapons in the text these methods are covered briefly, however, a few additional comments may further enlighten the reader.

Generally speaking, Civil War era firearms attained ignition in one of three different ways: flint and steel, percussion primers, or internally primed cartridges.

Flint and Steel

This method was outdated long before the Civil War, but the need for serviceable arms at the onset, brought many flintlock guns out of storage before they could be altered to the newer percussion system. Flintlocks were developed during the early 1600s to replace several other cumbersome arrangements. This system employed a piece of flint (a hard quartz-like stone) that was clamped into the top of the musket hammer. When fired, the hammer fell forward and drove the flint into a vertical, spring-held piece of steel called a frizzen. The frizzen served a dual purpose: when not being actively used, it was a cover for a small "pan" that contained a priming charge of about ten grains of black powder. In operation, when the flint struck the frizzen, the frizzen snapped back exposing the priming charge at the same time a shower of sparks fell into the pan. The sparks ignited the priming charge and passed fire through a small hole in the side of the barrel that communicated with the main powder charge in the barrel. The system worked well when it worked, but was very prone to misfires. The failure of the sparks to ignite the priming charge, a damp priming charge, or a lost priming charge were just some of the reasons the flintlock system was less than adequate.

Percussion Primers

The principal means of ignition in Civil War small arms was the percussion system that used the copper percussion cap. The device is popularly credited to the Englishman, Joshua Shaw, who was issued a U.S. patent in 1822. For shoulder arms, the percussion cap looked like a tiny "top hat" and was about the size of a modern pencil eraser. Pistol caps were usually straight-sided without the "brim" and were smaller still. The interior of the percussion cap had a small deposit of fulminate of mercury or another "salt" formed by dissolving a metal in acid. The correct formula produced a substance that exploded when it was struck a sharp blow. After loading the weapon with powder and ball or an externally primed cartridge, a percussion cap was placed by hand onto a hollow tube, called a cone or nipple, at the breech end

Musket flint (left) and another covered with a strip of lead to help hold it in the hammer's jaws (right).

Musket caps (top) and pistol caps (bottom).

of the barrel. When the hammer was tripped it fell onto the percussion cap. The exploding cap shot a concentrated flame into the barrel or a chamber and ignited the powder charge. Percussion caps were a great improvement over the old flint and steel method, but they did require some amount of manual dexterity in handling. In the Federal service twelve percussion caps were packaged in each bundle of ten cartridges; for quality reasons, the Confederates usually packaged thirteen caps. Each round or charge to be fired needed a new cap. A related complaint about this system was the failure of the mainspring to drop the hammer with sufficient force to explode the cap. This ailment was more notable among some patented carbines and imported arms.

Methods to improve on the percussion cap began soon after its adoption by the United States in the early 1840s. Edward Maynard was issued a patent for his percussion tape primers on September 22, 1845. The invention, very similar to present-day rolls of caps for toy guns, was purchased by the U.S. Ordnance Department for use with its Model of 1855 arms, and other weapons were altered for its employment. In Maynard's idea, small pellets of fulminate were cemented between two strips of paper and then shellacked for moisture resistance. A coil of forty primers was placed in a special compartment in the lockplate and were fed out over the cone one at a time by cocking the hammer. The lockplate and hammer were so arranged that when the hammer was tripped it cut off the exposed primer from the strip and ignited it on the cone. Although the Maynard tape primers themselves cost only 33 cents per thousand to manufacture at the Frankford Arsenal in 1859, the Civil War emergency created the Model of 1861 rifle musket that was quicker and cheaper to make than the M1855 because it eliminated the Maynard primer mechanism. By mid-May 1861, Federal arsenals were ordered to no longer issue tape primers and to package only percussion caps with their ammunition.

On June 28, 1853, Christian Sharps, of Sharps carbine and rifle fame, was issued a patent for an improved percussion "disc" primer that was adapted to the small arms of his name. The primer was made of two thin copper discs that encased a fulminate charge. About twenty-five primers were packaged with a wooden spacer in a open-sided brass sleeve. The spacer served to push the primers into a special mechanism or magazine located behind the breech and on top of the lockplate of several models. Hammer action ejected one disc at a time just in time to be

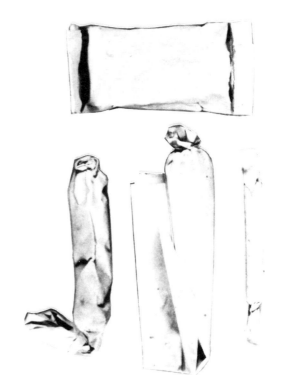

Packages of percussion caps, far right for revolver.

Maynard tape primers and lids from cans.

Sharps primers and lid from can.

73

crushed and exploded on the weapon's cone. A later modification to the mechanism allowed the magazine to be "cut-off" so the user could employ regulation percussion caps while the magazine remained in reserve. The Federal government purchased only about 2,000,000 Sharps primers at various times during the Civil War.

Internally Primed Cartridges

The most advanced form of ignition used in Civil War weapons was the internally primed cartridge. Here the primer, powder charge and bullet were combined in one unit or cartridge that was virtually impervious to moisture. A soldier was not required to prime the weapon with loose powder or handle a separate small primer. The gun could be quickly loaded in one motion and thus the rate of fire was dramatically increased. Two kinds of internally primed cartridges, the rimfire and pinfire, have been discussed in our *Ammunition* section. A third kind worth mentioning was a primitive form of the modern centerfire. On June 29, 1858, George Washington Morse of Baton Rouge, Louisiana was issued a patent for an improvement in cartridges that had all the features of an internally primed cartridge. Morse devised a hollow copper or brass cartridge case with a perforated "anvil" secured inside near the base. A standard percussion cap was placed on the anvil and the base was sealed with a rubberized "donut" leaving the flat portion of the cap exposed. The prepared case was charged with powder and a bullet inserted in the open end. Basically, a "firing pin" in the breech of the weapon was driven forward by the hammer. When the pin struck the center of the cartridge it exploded the cap and in turn the powder charge. It was claimed that the cases were reusable. The U.S. Ordnance Department was impressed enough with the system to have trial guns and ammunition prepared, but before any conclusive tests were done the Civil War began. Morse sided with the Confederacy and soon developed a new breechloading carbine for his ammunition. Perhaps as many as 1,000 carbines were produced during the war at various locations in the South. The weapon and its unique cartridges saw limited use, but are known to have been used in the Battle of Bentonville, North Carolina and elsewhere.

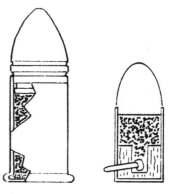

Cutaway drawings of a Spencer rimfire cartridge (left) and a pinfire cartridge (right).

Confederate Morse carbine cartridge.

Loading and Firing

The procedures below for loading and firing an infantry musket, the Sharps carbine, and a Colt revolver are taken from various Civil War era "Manuals of Arms." Should anyone be considering shooting an antique weapon, it must first be thoroughly checked by a qualified gunsmith, and then operated only in a safe area using black powder.

INFANTRY MUSKET

1. LOAD. *(Two motions.)*

One. Drop the piece by a smart extension of the left arm, seize it with the right hand above and near the tail band; at the same time carry the right foot forward, the heel against the hollow of the left foot.

Two. Drop the piece with the right hand along the left thigh, seize it with the left hand at the middle band, and with the left hand let it descend along to the ground, without shock, the piece touching the left thigh, and the muzzle opposite to the centre of the body; carry the right hand quickly to the cartridge-box and open it.

2. Handle-CARTRIDGE. *(One motion.)*

Seize the cartridge with the thumb and next two fingers, and place it between the teeth.

3. Tear-CARTRIDGE. *(One motion.)*

Tear the paper down to the powder, hold the cartridge upright between the thumb and next two fingers, near the top; and in this position place it in front of and near the muzzle, the back of the hand to the front.

4. Charge-CARTRIDGE. *(One motion.)*

Fix the eye on the muzzle, turn quickly the back of the right hand towards the body, in order to discharge the powder into the barrel, raise the elbow to the height of the wrist, shake the cartridge, force it into the muzzle and leave the hand reversed, the fingers extended, the thumb extended along the barrel.

5. Draw-RAMMER. *(Three motions.)*

One. Drop smartly the right elbow and seize the rammer between the thumb and forefinger bent, the other fingers shut; draw it smartly extending the arm; seize the rammer again at the middle, between the thumb and forefinger, the hand reversed, the palm to the front, the nails up, the eyes following the movement of the hand; clear the rammer from the pipes by again extending the arm.

75

Two. Turn rapidly the rammer between the bayonet and the face, closing the fingers, (the rammer of the rear rank man grazing the right shoulder of the man of the same file in front, respectively) the rammer parallel to the bayonet, the arm extended, the butt of the rammer opposite to the muzzle, but not yet inserted, the eyes fixed on the muzzle.

Three. Insert the butt of the rammer and force it down as low as the hand.

6. Ram-CARTRIDGE. *(One motion.)*

Extend the arm to its full length to seize the rammer between the right thumb extended and the forefinger bent, the other fingers closed; with force ram home twice (the right elbow down and near the piece) and seize the rammer at the little end, between the thumb and forefinger bent, the other fingers closed, the right elbow touching the body.

7. Return-RAMMER. *(Three motions.)*

One. Draw briskly the rammer, reseize it at the middle between the thumb and forefinger, the hand reversed, the palm to the front, the nails up, the eyes following the movement of the hand, clear the rammer from the barrel by extending the arm.

Two. Turn rapidly the rammer between the bayonet and the face, closing the fingers, (the rammer of the rear rank man grazing the right shoulder of the man of the same file in front,) the rammer parallel to the bayonet, the arm extended, the little end of the rammer opposite to the first pipe, but not yet inserted, the eyes fixed on that pipe.

Three. Insert the little end, and with the thumb, which will follow the movement, force it as low as the middle band; raise quickly the right hand a little bent, place the little finger on the butt of the rammer, and force it down: lower the left hand on the barrel to the extent of the arm, without depressing the shoulder.

8. Cast-ABOUT. *(Two motions.)*

One. Raise the piece with the left hand along the left side, the hand at the height of the chin, the forearm touching the piece, the barrel to the front; drop at the same time the right hand to seize the piece a little above the small, the forefinger touching the lock, the thumb on the S plate, and bring back the right heel to the side of the left.

Two. Make a half face to the right on the left heel, bring the left toe to the front, the right foot behind and at right-angles with the left, the hollow of the right foot against the heel of the left. At the same time seize the small of the stock with the right hand, and bring down the piece with both hands to the position of

charge-BAYONET.

9. PRIME.*(One motion.)*

Sustain the piece with left hand (half-cock the piece), brush off the old cap, and with the thumb and first two fingers take a cap from the pouch, place it firmly on the cone, pushing it down with the thumb.

If the gun was to be discharged, the commands were given:

1. *Ready*

The musket was brought to the front of the body at waist height, with the barrel pointing to the front. The hammer was positioned on full cock.

2. *Aim*

The butt of the musket was placed against the shoulder, the forefinger was placed on the trigger, and the sights were lined up on the target.

3. *Fire*

The trigger was pulled and the weapon fired. The soldier remained in his position until the next commands to reload or order arms.

SHARPS CARBINE

1. Load. *(Two motions.)*

One. At the command LOAD, make a half face to the right, turning on the left heel, bringing the toes of the left foot directly to the front, carry the right foot to the rear, the hollow of it opposite to, and 3 inches from, the left heel; detach the carbine perpendicularly four inches from the shoulder, raise it, and seize it with the left hand at the sight, the left forearm horizontal.

Two. Lower the muzzle to the height of the eye, the left hand as high as, and opposite to, the right breast, the thumb extended along the barrel; move back the catch with the forefinger of the right hand, seize the lever with the thumb and first two fingers, and throw it open to its full extent, and carry the right hand to the cartridge box and open it.

2. Charge-CARTRIDGE. *(Two motions.)*

One. At the command CARTRIDGE, draw the cartridge, insert it (ball foremost) in the barrel, press it in with the thumb and forefinger, and seize the lever with the thumb and first two fingers.

Two. Draw back the lever, move up the catch, half cock, remove the old cap and carry the hand to the cap pouch and open it.

3. PRIME.

At the command PRIME, place a cap on the cone, press it down with the thumb, let down the cock and seize the carbine at the small of the stock with the right hand.

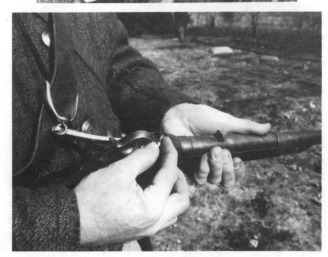

The carbine could now be fired on these commands:
1. *Ready*

One. At the command READY, make a half face to the right, carrying the right foot square behind the left, the hollow of it opposite to, and 3 inches from, the left heel; detach the carbine vertically four inches from the shoulder, seize it with the left hand a little below the band, the thumb along the stock, raise it with both hands, the left as high as the neck; place the right thumb upon the head of the hammer, the forefinger on the guard, the second finger under it, the elbow as high as the hand.

Two. Cock the piece by lowering quickly the right elbow, and seize the small of the stock.

2. *Aim*

At the command AIM, lower the muzzle quickly, the carbine resting between the thumb and first finger, the remaining fingers closed and under the stock, shut the left eye, direct the right eye along the barrel to aim, and place the forefinger of the right hand on the trigger.

3. *Fire*

At the command FIRE, pull the trigger and, fire without lowering or turning the head, and remain in this position.

COLT REVOLVER

Draw - PISTOL.

At the command PISTOL, pass the right hand between the bridle arm and the body, unbutton the pistol holster, seize the pistol at the butt, draw it, elevate it, the hammer as high as, and opposite to, the right shoulder, the muzzle up, the guard to the front, the forefinger over the guard.

1. LOAD

One. At the command LOAD, pass the pistol into the left bridle hand, muzzle up, guard diagonally towards the right, the little finger under the butt, the forefinger under the guard, at the same time place the thumb of the right hand on the hammer, the fingers of the right hand over three of the left.

Two. Half cock the pistol and carry the right hand to the cartridge box, and open it, at the same time raise the thumb of the left hand on the cylinder.

2. Handle-CARTRIDGE.

At the command CARTRIDGE, carry the cartridge to the mouth, tear off the paper to the powder, place the cartridge near the chamber which shows itself towards the face, holding it upwards between the thumb and first two fingers.

3. Charge-CARTRIDGE.

One. At the command CARTRIDGE, empty the powder into the chamber, carry the hand to the mouth, tear off the paper from the ball, place the ball in the chamber, and press it down with the thumb.

Two. Turn the cylinder with the left thumb until the ball is under the lever, seize at the same time the lever at the clasp, between the thumb and first finger of the right hand and loosen it from the catch.

4. Ram-CARTRIDGE.

At the command CARTRIDGE, ram the ball home, leave the lever in the cylinder, and carry the right hand to the cartridge box.

This process will be continued until all the chambers are loaded. When the last ball has been rammed home, throw up the lever and clasp it, revolve the cylinder until it clicks, and carry the hand to the cap pouch.

[Combustible cartridges greatly simplified the loading process for revolvers, especially when on horseback.]

5. PRIME.

One. At the command PRIME, drop the muzzle of the pistol towards the ground on the right side of the horse's neck, the wrist near the body, the back of the hand down, remove the thumb from the cylinder, carry a cap to the exposed cone and press it on with the thumb; turn the cylinder with the right hand until it clicks and carry the hand to the cap pouch.

This process will be continued until all the cones are capped. When the last cap has been placed on elevate the muzzle and take the first position of load, except that the forefinger is on the trigger.

Two. Let down the hammer on the safety notch and resume the position of *Draw Pistol.*

Ready

Drop the pistol between the thumb and first finger of the left hand, guard to the front, the muzzle diagonally to the left, at the same time place the right thumb on the hammer, the remaining fingers of the right hand closed and under the guard. Cock the pistol and resume the position of *Draw Pistol.*

Aim

At the command AIM, drop the muzzle to the front, extend the right arm and point the pistol at the target.

Fire

At the command FIRE, pull the trigger and at once resume the position of *Draw Pistol.*

Glossary

Army and Navy Caliber Revolvers—The terms *"Army"* and *"Navy,"* when associated with Civil War revolvers, can appear misleading. "Army" and "Navy" refer only to the caliber of an arm and in no way indicate its use by a particular branch of the armed forces. Army caliber revolvers are .44 caliber and Navy caliber revolvers are .36 cal. As nearly as can be determined, the terms originated with master salesman, Samuel Colt, in an attempt to enhance the sales of his arms to the two branches of the service.

Breechloading—The *breechloading* system allowed both projectile and gunpowder to be inserted into the arm through the breech or back end of the barrel. Breechloading significantly decreased loading time. This was a major advantage during the heat of battle.

Caliber—The inside diameter of a gun barrel measured in thousandths of an inch.

Carbine—The *carbine* is the shoulder arm of the cavalry. Because it was intended to be carried, and if necessary, used on horseback, the average length of the Civil War carbine was 39 inches. Loading a muzzleloading arm when on horseback is extremely difficult, if not almost impossible. For this reason most inventions of breechloading weapons were carbines. An inventor wishing to sell a new breechloading arm had a much better chance to do so if it was offered for cavalry use.

Cavalry—Soldiers who served on horseback.

Infantry—Soldiers who served on foot.

Lever-action Arms—*Lever-action arms* are breechloading firearms that employ a lever as an integral part of the arm. The lever opens the breech to allow either manual or mechanical insertion of a cartridge.

Magazine-fed Arms—In firearms terminology, a *magazine* is an ammunition storage place and an integral part of the arm. The magazine contains a spring and a follower to automatically force one cartridge at a time into the firing chamber. Two magazine-fed arms saw extensive use in the Civil War, the Henry rifle with its fifteen cartridge magazine and the Spencer (carbine or rifle) with its seven cartridge magazine.

Mounted Infantry—Soldiers who used horses for rapid movement, but were expected to fight on foot.

Musket—A *musket* is a smoothbore shoulder arm which fires a round lead ball. Smoothbore arms were standard issue in the U.S. Army until 1855, when they were replaced by a new model arm with a rifled bore. Although obsolete by the Civil War, many muskets were still in arsenal storage or in the hands of state militia units. In 1861, the average musket was 57 inches long and weighed about 9 pounds.

Muzzleloading—The *muzzleloading* system requires both the gunpowder and projectile to be inserted into the arm through the muzzle or front end of the barrel. Muzzleloading weapons were the standard issue to soldiers worldwide prior to and during the American Civil War.

Percussion Arms—*Percussion* means "striking" in music as well as in weaponry. Civil War small arms commonly used a small brass "cap" which contained a small amount of fulminate of mercury, a very volatile substance, to ignite the gunpowder charge which fired the weapon. A cap was placed on a cone or "nipple" that was mounted on the firearm in an area directly adjacent to the chamber. When loaded, the chamber contained the charge of black gunpowder necessary to fire the bullet. The cap was the striking point of the firearm's hammer. The resulting percussion of the hammer strike caused the fulminate to explode, sending a tiny flame through a hole in the cone and into the powder charge. About 100 of these caps could be carried in a small leather pouch attached to a soldier's belt. Each bullet fired required a new cap.

Pistol—A *pistol* is a hand-held firearm. At the time of the Civil War most pistols were revolvers, however, a few single-shot muzzleloading varieties remained in use.

Ranges of Small Arms—Most rifled Civil War shoulder arms, including carbines, could be fired with precision at ranges of 100 to 150 yards and with reasonable accuracy at distances of 200 to 300 yards. The rifle musket was effective for up to 1,000 yards, but at that range the chances of an aimed shot hitting even a very large target were no better than 50/50. The accuracy of smoothbore shoulder arms was very good at 50 to 100 yards, but began to drop off rapidly after that distance. Precision shooting with Civil War revolvers was possible for up to 50 yards and the accuracy needed to hit a man-sized target was present for up to 150 yards.

Rate of Fire—*Rate of fire* is defined as the number of times a user can load, aim, and fire a gun in a given period of time (usually one minute). During the Civil War, all comparisons were made with the rifle musket as the standard. An increased rate of fire was the objective of most improvements to firearms during the war. An experienced soldier could achieve the following rates of fire:
Rifled musket: 2-3 shots per minute
Single-shot breechloader: 10 shots per minute
Magazine-fed repeater: Spencer: 20 shots per minute
Henry: 30 shots per minute

Regular Army—The *Regular Army* refers to the standing army, raised and permanently maintained by an existing national government. Prior to the Civil War the Regular Army of the United States consisted only of four regiments of cavalry, four regiments of artillery and ten regiments of infantry.

Revolver—A *revolver* is hand-held firearm which includes a cylinder with a number of chambers (usually 6) containing cartridges. The cartridges were fired one at a time. During the Civil War, revolvers were issued primarily to cavalrymen, although some light artillerymen also carried them. Because of its convenient size and weight, the revolver was the weapon preferred by most officers.

Rifle—The *rifle* is a shoulder arm with a rifled bore. In the mid-19th century, the rifle was distinguished from the musket or rifle-musket by its length, which was usually about 49 inches. The shorter length of the rifle was ideal for mounted infantry troops or troops serving as skirmishers, where added maneuverability was important. When breechloading infantry arms were introduced at the time of the Civil War, the length of the rifle was considered to be perfect. These breechloading rifles also offered increased loading speed.

Rifled Bore Arms—Rifling in firearms consists of cutting an evenly spaced number of spiral grooves in the inner surface of the barrel (bore). These grooves caused a projectile passing through the barrel to spin on its axis, thereby greatly increasing its accuracy. The United States Regular Army was not totally equipped with rifled small arms until after 1855.

Rifle-Musket—The *rifle-musket* is a shoulder arm with a length of about 56 inches. which was manufactured with a rifled bore. The United States adopted its first rifle-musket in 1855. It quickly replaced the common musket as standard issue to the Regular Army. The model 1855 rifle-musket fired a new bullet shaped projectile known as the Minie ball. Its high degree of accuracy was a factor in the Civil War.

Rifled Musket—The *rifled musket* is a rifled shoulder arm which was originally manufactured with a smooth bore. When small arms with rifled bores became general issue in the U. S. Army after 1855, small arms with smooth bores became obsolete. As an economy measure, many of the stockpiles of smoothbore muskets on hand were sent back to various manufacturing points to have rifling grooves cut into the bore. These rifled muskets were issued to militia units or placed in storage for an emergency.

Sharpshooter—A *sharpshooter* was the Civil War era sniper. Although some sharpshooters used the rifle manufactured by the Sharps Rifle Company, there is no evidence that there is any connection between that rifle company and sharpshooter designations as such.

Shoulder Arm—*Shoulder arms* are those whose length and weight are such that they must be supported against the shoulder and held with both hands to be fired. During the Civil War, shoulder arms nearly always fired a larger bullet and used a much greater powder charge than hand-held weapons such as revolvers. This increased powder charge and longer barrel gave projectiles fired from shoulder arms a greater effective range than those fired from revolvers.

Single or Double-Action Arms—*Single* and *double action* applies to arms which employ a revolving cylinder as a cartridge storage area. These arms all employ a small striking arm (called a hammer) to ignite the cartridge. Single-action mechanisms require the user to manually cock (set) the hammer each time a cartridge is to be fired. The cocking of the hammer causes the cylinder to turn one step and aligns the chamber containing the next cartridge with the barrel. The user then pulls the trigger to release the hammer and fire the weapon. Double-action arms allow the user to automatically turn the cylinder, set the hammer, and release the hammer by simply pulling the trigger. Double-action mechanisms were more complicated and consequently more expensive. Despite its advantages, use of double-action revolvers was very limited during the Civil War.

Smoothbore Arms—*Smoothbore arms* are those in which the inner surface of the barrel (bore) is entirely smooth. These arms fired a round lead ball which was cast slightly smaller than the diameter of the bore. This allowed the ball to be rammed down the barrel in preparation for firing. The ball would rest on the gunpowder charge which, when ignited, forced the ball out of the barrel. Smoothbore arms were used by the U. S. Army from the Revolution until the late 1850s. The greatly increased accuracy of arms with rifled bores made smoothbore arms obsolete.

Volunteers—Volunteer soldiers made up the vast majority of both the Union and Confederate armies. These soldiers enlisted (volunteered) for military service strictly because of the war emergency. Unlike the regular army, their term of service was expected to last only as long as the war itself.

Soldiers with non-regulation revolvers: Model 1855 Colt "Root" (left) and Uhlinger (right).

84

Appendix A

Federal and Northern State Arsenals

The U.S. Ordnance Department facilities and northern state operations at the following locations provided the vast majority of ammunition supplied to Federal troops. However, not listed here are many private cartridge makers who had contracts with the government from time to time. In total, from January 1, 1861, to June 30, 1866, the Ordnance Department provided 1,022,176,474 cartridges for small arms.

Federal Arsenals
Allegheny, (Pittsburgh) Pennsylvania
Benicia, California
Columbus, Ohio
Fort Monroe, Virginia
Frankford, (Philadelphia) Pennsylvania
Kennebec, (Augusta) Maine
Leavenworth, Kansas
St. Louis, Missouri
Vancouver, Washington Territory
Washington, District of Columbia
Watertown, Massachusetts
Watervliet, (W. Troy) New York

State Arsenals
Indianapolis, Indiana
Frankfurt, Kentucky
Columbus, Ohio
Albany, New York

Appendix B

Confederate Arsenals, Depots and Laboratories

Ammunition for small arms is known to have been manufactured at the following southern locations. Other establishments such as the sites at New Iberia, Louisiana and Marshall, Texas apparently had some production for a time.

Atlanta, Georgia
Augusta, Georgia
Charleston, South Carolina
Columbus, Georgia
Columbus, Mississippi
Danville, Virginia
Fayetteville, North Carolina
Jackson, Mississippi
Little Rock, Arkansas

Lynchburg, Virginia
Macon, Georgia
Mt. Vernon, Alabama
Nashville, Tennessee
New Orleans, Louisiana
Richmond, Virginia
San Antonio, Texas
Savannah, Georgia
Selma, Alabama

Appendix C

Small Arms Usage by Regiments

The regimental small arms listings presented here are intended to give the reader an idea of who actually carried these arms into battle. The lists were compiled from ordnance returns and ammunition requisitions found in Record Groups 94, 109 and 156 in the National Archives and Records Administration, Washington, D.C.

In general, the lists represent the 1863-64 time period. Because many regiments exchanged small arms at least once during the war, the listings may not be valid for the entire length of service of all regiments. This is particularly true of Union cavalry regiments, many of whom were issued Spencer carbines near the end of the war.

Confederate ordnance returns exist, but are scattered and often incomplete. It is believed that the information found here is representative of the general issue of arms by the Confederacy.

Regiments carrying more than one type of weapon were common in both armies. For this reason a special listing called "Mixed Model 1861s and Enfield Rifle Muskets" is presented and/or a regiment may be found listed under more than one type of arm.

Flintlock Muskets .69 cal.
C.S.
23 VA (1861)
25 VA (1861)

Smoothbore Model 1842 .69 cal.
U.S.

7 IA	4 NY H.A.
1 KS Col.	9 NY H.A.
20 KY	4 OH
18 ME	33 PA
23 ME	34 PA
26 ME	36 PA
9 MA	40 PA
11 MA	41 PA
42 MA	55 PA
50 MA	81 PA
12 NH	90 PA
7 NJ	93 PA
11 NJ	102 PA
12 NJ	116 PA
63 NY	138 PA
69 NY	145 PA
88 NY	155 PA
133 NY	168 PA
139 NY	11 WI
158 NY	1 US C.T.
170 NY	74 US C.T.

Smoothbore Muskets .69 cal.
C.S.

24 Bn. GA Cav	5 TX
38 GA	8 TX Cav
4 NC	23 VA (1861)
13 NC	33 VA
22 NC	44 VA (1861)
38 NC	
1 SC Rifles	
4 TN	
1 TX	
4 TX	

Model 1842 Rifled Muskets .69 cal.
U.S.

3 DE	30 PA
59 IL	31 PA
111 IL	38 PA
114 IL	79 PA
115 IL	93 PA
35 IA	139 PA
20 KY	1 WI
9 ME	4 WI
21 MO	10 WI
23 MO	11 WI
35 MO	19 WI
1 NE	20 WI
47 NY	
61 OH	C.S.
11 PA	2 NC Cav

Rifled Muskets altered to percussion .69 cal.
U.S.
87 IL
88 IL
91 IL
103 IL
122 IL
129 IL

Smoothbore Muskets altered to percussion .69 cal.

U.S.	C.S.
171 PA	23 VA (1861)
172 PA	25 VA (1861)
	37 VA (1861)
	44 VA (1861)

Austrian, Prussian or French Smoothbore Muskets
U.S.
174 PA
34 WI
34 US C.T.

Model 1855 or Model 1861 Rifle Muskets .58 cal.
U.S.

1 CA	7 MD	11 NJ	62 OH
2 CA	Purnell Legion MD	14 NJ	66 OH
3 CA	1 MA	10 NY	67 OH
4 CA	5 MA	40 NY	69 OH
5 CA	15 MA	41 NY	76 OH
6 CA	17 MA	44 NY	79 OH
2 CO	18 MA	49 NY	89 OH
3 CO	22 MA	52 NY	91 OH
5 CT	24 MA	56 NY	92 OH
8 CT	26 MA	65 NY	93 OH
11 CT	29 MA	67 NY	98 NY
13 CT	34 MA	68 NY	101 OH
14 CT	37 MA	70 NY	102 OH
15 CT	39 MA	71 NY	105 OH
18 CT	40 MA	72 NY	107 OH
20 CT	41 MA	73 NY	110 OH
21 CT	45 MA	75 NY	111 OH
22 CT	52 MA	76 NY	113 OH
1 CT H.A.	14 MA H.A.	82 NY	116 OH
27 CT	1 MA Bat. H.A.	83 NY	121 OH
1 DE	1 Unat. Co. MA H.A.	84 NY	123 OH
2 DE	1 MI	94 NY	124 OH
4 DE	2 MI	95 NY	125 OH
16 IL	4 MI	102 NY	29 PA
19 IL	7 MI	107 NY	32 PA
53 IL	11 MI	108 NY	35 PA
78 IL	13 MI	109 NY	37 PA
83 IL	16 MI	111 NY	45 PA
89 IL	17 MI	114 NY	46 PA
9 IN	18 MI	117 NY	47 PA
13 IN	20 MI	120 NY	53 PA
19 IN	24 MI	123 NY	56 PA
27 IN	1 MI S.S.	125 NY	61 PA
50 IN	1 MN	126 NY	62 PA
75 IN	6 MN	127 NY	71 PA
80 IN	7 MN	134 NY	74 PA
101 IN	8 MN	142 NY	75 PA
2 IA	9 MN	143 NY	83 PA
6 IA	10 MN	145 NY	91 PA
15 IA	29 MO	146 NY	95 PA
16 IA	MS Marine Brig.	169 NY	97 PA
8 KS	2 NH	7 NY H.A.	100 PA
10 KS	10 NH	8 NY H.A.	105 PA
13 KY	11 NH	5 OH	106 PA
14 KY	12 NH	7 OH	109 PA
20 KY	13 NH	9 OH	114 PA
22 KY	14 NH	11 OH	118 PA
3 ME	1 NJ	14 OH	119 PA
5 ME	2 NJ	17 OH	121 PA
6 ME	3 NJ	27 OH	140 PA
7 ME	4 NJ	32 OH	141 PA
10 ME	6 NJ	35 OH	148 PA
11 ME	8 NJ	41 OH	26 PA Mil.
19 ME	9 NJ	52 OH	27 PA Mil.

28 PA Mil.	4 US	117 IL	93 IN
29 PA Mil.	5 US	118 IL	97 IN
1 PA Em. Bn.	6 US	119 IL	99 IN
2 RI	7 US	124 IL	100 IN
12 RI	8 US	125 IL	3 IA
1 TN	9 US	126 IL	4 IA
2 VT	10 US	127 IL	8 IA
3 VT	11 US	130 IL	11 IA
5 VT	12 US	131 IL	12 IA
7 VT	13 US	6 IN	13 IA
10 VT	14 US	7 IN	14 IA
12 VT	15 US	10 IN	17 IA
13 VT	16 US	12 IN	18 IA
15 VT	17 US	16 IN	19 IA
16 VT	18 US	18 IN	20 IA
3 WI	19 US	20 IN	21 IA
6 WI		22 IN	22 IA
8 WI	C.S.	23 IN	23 IA
17 WI	21 MS	24 IN	24 IA
29 WI	4 NC	25 IN	25 IA
1 US	38 NC	26 IN	26 IA
2 US	41 TN	29 IN	27 IA
3 US		30 IN	28 IA
		31 IN	29 IA
Enfield Rifle Musket .577 cal.		32 IN	30 IA
U.S.		33 IN	31 IA
6 CT	52 IL	34 IN	32 IA
7 CT	54 IL	35 IN	33 IA
9 CT	57 IL	36 IN	34 IA
10 CT	60 IL	37 IN	39 IA
12 CT	63 IL	38 IN	40 IA
16 CT	65 IL	39 IN	11 KS
17 CT	72 IL	40 IN	12 KS
19 CT	73 IL	42 IN	13 KS
23 CT	74 IL	43 IN	2 KY
24 CT	75 IL	44 IN	3 KY
25 CT	76 IL	47 IN	4 KY
26 CT	77 IL	52 IN	5 KY
28 CT	81 IL	54 IN	6 KY
7 IL	82 IL	57 IN	7 KY
8 IL	84 IL	58 IN	8 KY
10 IL	85 IL	59 IN	9 KY
11 IL	86 IL	60 IN	10 KY
20 IL	90 IL	63 IN	12 KY
21 IL	92 IL	66 IN	15 KY
22 IL	93 IL	67 IN	16 KY
23 IL	94 IL	68 IN	17 KY
25 IL	95 IL	69 IN	19 KY
26 IL	96 IL	70 IN	21 KY
27 IL	97 IL	71 IN	26 KY
28 IL	100 IL	79 IN	27 KY
30 IL	104 IL	84 IN	1 LA
31 IL	107 IL	85 IN	2 LA
46 IL	110 IL	86 IN	1 LA Art.
48 IL	113 IL	88 IN	8 ME
49 IL	116 IL	89 IN	12 ME

13 ME	31 MO	153 NY	74 OH
15 ME	32 MO	154 NY	75 OH
16 ME	33 MO	155 NY	78 OH
17 ME	3 NH	156 NY	81 OH
21 ME	5 NH	157 NY	82 OH
24 ME	7 NH	159 NY	83 OH
27 ME	8 NH	160 NY	90 OH
28 ME	15 NH	161 NY	92 OH
1 ME H.A.	16 NH	164 NY	94 OH
1 MD	10 NJ	165 NY	95 OH
2 MD	15 NJ	173 NY	97 OH
4 MD	3 NY	174 NY	99 OH
6 MD	15 NY	175 NY	100 OH
8 MD	46 NY	176 NY	103 OH
1 MD P.H.B.	48 NY	177 NY	104 OH
3 MD P.H.B.	51 NY	178 NY	106 OH
1 MD E.S.	54 NY	1 NY Eng.	107 OH
2 MD E.S.	57 NY	69 NY N.G.	117 OH
2 MA	58 NY	2 NY H.A.	118 OH
4 MA	61 NY	5 NY H.A.	122 OH
7 MA	66 NY	6 NY H.A.	Pioneer Brig. OH
10 MA	74 NY	10 NY H.A.	27 PA
12 MA	77 NY	1 OH	39 PA
13 MA	78 NY	2 OH	48 PA
16 MA	79 NY	4 OH	51 PA
19 MA	81 NY	8 OH	68 PA
20 MA	86 NY	10 OH	73 PA
23 MA	90 NY	13 OH	76 PA
25 MA	91 NY	15 OH	78 PA
27 MA	92 NY	18 OH	82 PA
28 MA	93 NY	19 OH	85 PA
30 MA	96 NY	20 OH	87 PA
31 MA	97 NY	21 OH	88 PA
32 MA	104 NY	23 OH	96 PA
33 MA	106 NY	25 OH	107 PA
35 MA	110 NY	26 OH	111 PA
36 MA	112 NY	29 OH	115 PA
38 MA	115 NY	30 OH	142 PA
48 MA	116 NY	36 OH	143 PA
49 MA	118 NY	37 OH	147 PA
53 MA	119 NY	38 OH	149 PA
54 MA	122 NY	42 OH	150 PA
55 MA	124 NY	45 OH	151 PA
10 MI	128 NY	47 OH	157 PA
19 MI	130 NY	48 OH	165 PA
25 MI	131 NY	49 OH	166 PA
26 MI	136 NY	50 OH	167 PA
27 MI	137 NY	51 OH	169 PA
1 MI Eng. & Mech.	141 NY	55 OH	173 PA
3 MN	144 NY	56 OH	177 PA
3 MO	147 NY	58 OH	178 PA
6 MO	148 NY	59 OH	179 PA
7 MO	149 NY	68 OH	5 RI
8 MO	150 NY	70 OH	7 RI
11 MO	151 NY	72 OH	11 RI
30 MO	152 NY	73 OH	2 TN

3 TN	23 WI
4 TN	24 WI
4 VT	25 WI
6 VT	26 WI
8 VT	27 WI
9 VT	28 WI
2 VA	31 WI
4 VA	32 WI
5 VA	33 WI
6 VA	35 US C.T.
9 VA	48 US C.T.
10 VA	73 US C.T.
11 VA	74 US C.T.
12 VA	
14 VA	C.S.
15 VA	2 NC Cav
4 WI	60 NC
8 WI	4 TN
11 WI	4 TX
14 WI	9 TX
16 WI	11 VA Cav
18 WI	

Mixed Model 1861 and Enfield Rifle Muskets

U.S.

12 IL	MO Eng.
13 IL	13 NJ
15 IL	42 NY
17 IL	59 NY
18 IL	99 NY
24 IL	121 NY
50 IL	140 NY
79 IL	168 NY
105 IL	6 OH
8 IN	22 OH
11 IN	24 OH
14 IN	31 OH
15 IN	33 OH
46 IN	37 OH
24 KY	40 OH
20 ME	61 OH
25 ME	64 OH
3 MD	65 OH
21 MA	69 OH
3 MI	69 PA
6 MI	72 PA
8 MI	77 PA
23 MI	84 PA
2 MN	110 PA
15 MO	8 TN
17 MO	1 VA
24 MO	7 VA
25 MO	13 VA
26 MO	21 WI
27 MO	

C.S.

Cobb's Legion GA	17 MS
Phillip's Legion GA	18 MS
10 GA	21 MS
16 GA	15 NC
18 GA	2 SC
24 GA	3 SC
50 GA	8 SC
51 GA	15 SC
53 GA	1 TX
13 MS	5 TX

Enfield Rifles, saber bayonet, .577 cal.

U.S.	C.S.
11 IN	Cobb's Legion GA
25 IN	Phillip's Legion GA
53 IN	10 GA
63 IN	16 GA
20 IA	18 GA
60 NY	51 GA
132 NY	13 MS
Ind. Bn. NY	17 MS
39 OH	18 MS
81 OH	21 MS
28 PA	2 NC Cav
147 PA	2 SC
11 VA	41 TN
	1 Bn. TX S.S.
	5 TX
	7 VA Cav

Richmond Rifle Muskets .58 cal.

C.S.
16 VA Cav

Richmond Rifles .58 cal.

C.S.
21 MS
36 Bn. VA Cav

Fayetteville Rifles

C.S
9 TX

Austrian Rifle Muskets .54 cal.

U.S.

47 IL	87 IN
51 IL	18 IA
56 IL	30 IA
120 IL	36 IA
49 IN	38 IA

1 KY	126 OH
18 KY	23 PA
23 KY	26 PA
4 ME	49 PA
14 ME	54 PA
2 MD P.H.B.	57 PA
4 MA	58 PA
8 MA	63 PA
47 MA	99 PA
5 MI	101 PA
9 MI	103 PA
12 MI	104 PA
14 MI	107 PA
15 MI	141 PA
21 MI	4 RI
22 MI	5 TN
10 MO	6 TN
6 NH	10 TN
5 NJ	14 VT
43 NY	2 WI
50 NY	5 WI
62 NY	7 WI
64 NY	46 US C.T.
80 NY	48 US C.T.
85 NY	49 US C.T.
89 NY	51 US C.T.
103 NY	53 US C.T.
162 NY	75 US C.T.
46 OH	76 US C.T.
48 OH	
53 OH	C.S.
57 OH	40 GA
63 OH	41 GA
77 OH	43 GA
80 OH	52 GA
108 OH	2 NC Cav
114 OH	12 TN
115 OH	47 Tn
120 OH	8 TX Cav

Austrian Rifle Muskets .577 & .58 cal.

U.S.	
106 IL	176 PA
74 IN	11 VT
81 IN	7 WI
82 IN	9 WI
22 ME	47 US C.T.
43 MA	48 US C.T.
6 MI	59 US C.T.
98 NY	75 US C.T.
100 NY	
50 PA	C.S.
52 PA	29 TN
153 PA	
158 PA	

Austrian and Prussian Rifled Muskets .69 & .70 cal.

U.S.
37 IA
12 OH
88 OH
174 PA

Light French or "Liege" Rifles .577 cal.

U.S.
53 IN
39 NY
22 OH

French Rifle Muskets .58 cal.

U.S.	
43 IL	12 WI
41 IA	13 WI
98 PA	15 WI
9 WI	16 WI

Belgian or French Rifled Muskets .69 cal.

U.S.	71 OH
37 IL	96 OH
62 IL	9 WI
102 IL	33 US C.T.
108 IL	
2 MO	C.S.
12 MO	60 NC
4 NH	21 TN
16 OH	8 TX Cav

Belgian or Vincennes Rifles .70 & .71 cal.

U.S.
25 IN
83 IN
91 IN
132 NY
28 OH
54 OH

Dresden and Suhl Rifle Muskets .58 cal.

U.S.
44 IL
55 IL
9 IA
56 OH
22 WI
30 WI

Model 1841 "Mississippi" Rifle .54 cal.

U.S.
2 Indian Home Guard
46 MA
51 MA
9 NH
45 NY
15 NY H.A.
1 WA Terr.

1 MO Cav
3 SC
8 SC
15 SC
8 TX Cav
11 TX Cav
23 VA
12 VA Cav
14 VA Cav

C.S.
18 GA
21 MS

34 Bn. VA Cav
35 Bn. VA Cav
36 Bn. VA Cav

Model 1840/45 Rifles .58 cal.

U.S.
10 IL
42 IL
64 IL
11 IN
48 IN
3 Indian Home Guard
5 IA
10 IA

1 KS
8 KS
10 KS
4 MN
5 MN
1 MO
9 OH
39 OH

Whitworth Rifle

C.S.
4 NC (1)

Colt Revolving Rifles

Cavalry
U.S.
3 IL
7 IL
9 IL
15 IL
2 IN
2 IA
7 KS
1 KY
3 KY
4 KY
7 KY
26 KY Mtd. Inf
2 MI
3 MI
4 MI
1 MO
4 NY
2 OH
13 TN
3 US Colored

4 US

C.S.
12 VA

Infantry
U.S.
22 IL
27 IL
37 IL
42 IL
44 IL
51 IL
66 IL
73 IL
74 IL
98 IL
12 KY
26 KY
34 KY

9 OH
21 OH
26 OH
38 OH
21 MI
2 MN
13 MO
15 MO

17 MO
5 NH
1 US S.S.
2 US S.S.
7 US
8 US
9 US
10 US

Henry Rifles

Cavalry
U.S.
1 DC
12 KY
1 ME

16 IL
23 IL
51 IL
66 IL
80 IL
58 IN

Infantry
U.S.
7 IL

93 IN
97 IN
7 VA

Merrill Rifles

U.S.
1 IN H.A.
Andrew's S.S. MA

Sharps Rifles

U.S.
1 CT
2 CT
4 CT
6 CT
7 CT
8 CT
11 CT
13 CT
14 CT
66 IL
113 IL
20 IN
11 KY
12 KY
11 KY Mtd. Inf
3 MI
5 MI
16 MI
15 MA
Andrew's S.S. MA
1 MN
8 MN
26 MO
27 MO
2 NH
3 NH

30 NJ
2 NY
5 NY
146 NY
151 NY
1 NY Ind. S.S.
38 PA
42 PA
149 PA
150 PA
190 PA
4 WI
1 US S.S.
2 US S.S.
37 US C.T.

Spencer Rifles

Cavalry	
U.S.	102 IL
8 IN	123 IL
11 KY	13 IN
2 MA	17 IN
4 MA	20 IN
2 MI	40 IN
5 MI	72 IN
6 MI	97 IN
7 MI	4 KY
8 MI	28 KY
9 MI	37 MA
10 MI	54 MA
5 NY	57 MA
7 NY	14 MI
11 OH	24 MI
1 VA	27 MI
	3 NH
C.S.	10 NH
2 NC Cav	65 NY
8 TX	79 NY
	118 NY
Infantry	148 NY
U.S.	46 OH
7 CT	75 OH Mtd. Inf
1 DE	79 OH
9 IL	OH S.S.-5, 6, 7 & 8 Cos.
27 IL	105 PA
92 IL	148 PA
98 IL	190 PA
	37 US C.T.

Ballard Carbines

U.S.	4 KY Mtd. Inf
3 KY Cav	13 KY Mtd. Inf
6 KY Cav	30 KY Mtd. Inf
13 KY Cav	45 KY Mtd. Inf

Burnside Carbines

Cavalry	11 KY
U.S.	1 ME
2 IL	1 MI
3 IL	6 MO
6 IL	1 NJ
12 IL	1 NY Vet
14 IL	2 NY
16 IL	3 NY
3 IN	11 NY
3 IA	12 NY
1 KY	14 NY
5 KY	15 NY
6 KY	21 NY
7 KY	25 NY

1 OH	Loudon Rgrs VA
4 OH	3 WV
5 OH	2 WI
6 OH	4 WI
7 OH	
7 PA	C.S.
8 PA	2 NC
9 PA	8 TX
12 PA	6 VA
13 PA	7 VA
14 PA	11 VA
15 PA	12 VA
20 PA	35 Bn. VA

Cosmopolitan Carbines

Cavalry	
U.S.	8 IA
4 IL	14 KS
5 IL	14 KY
6 IL	8 MO
4 IA	8 OH

Gallager Carbines

Cavalry	1 NY
U.S.	9 OH
2 AR	10 OH
13 IL	20 PA
3 IN	21 PA
9 IN	1 TN
4 IA	2 TN
7 IA	8 TN
9 KS	9 TN
8 KY	
15 KY	C.S.
4 MO	11 VA

Gibbs Carbines

Cavalry
U.S.
10 MO
13 NY
16 NY

Hall Carbines

Cavalry	7 MO
U.S.	
Dakota Terr.	C.S.
3 IL	11 TX
11 IL	1 VA
1 IN	6 VA
2 MO	11 VA
6 MO	12 VA

Maynard Carbines

Cavalry	C.S.
U.S.	2 FL
6 IN	Cobb's Legion GA
9 IN	1 MS
11 IN	
10 TN	Infantry
11 TN	C.S.
	2 FL

Merrill Carbines

Cavalry	18 PA
U.S.	2 TN
1 DE	5 TN
7 IN	1 WI
2 KS	3 WI
5 KS	
14 KS	C.S.
11 MO	1 VA
1 NY	7 VA
5 NY	11 VA
18 NY	12 VA
5 PA	14 VA
11 PA	35 Bn. VA
17 PA	

Sharps Carbines

Cavalry	7 MO
U.S.	1 NY Mtd. Rifles
1 CA	2 NY
2 CA	3 NY
4 IL	4 NY
5 IL	6 NY
6 IL	8 NY
7 IL	9 NY
8 IL	13 NY
9 IL	16 NY
10 IL	1 OH
15 IL	3 OH
1 IA	1 PA
2 IA	2 PA
4 IA	3 PA
5 IA	4 PA
1 IN	5 PA
5 KS	6 PA
7 KS	8 PA
15 KS	15 PA
1 ME	16 PA
1 MA	1 RI
2 MA	3 TN
3 MA	6 TN
1 MD	12 TN
3 MO	1 VT

2 WI	C.S.
1 US	2 NC
2 US	1 VA
3 US	6 VA
5 US	7 VA
6 US	12 VA
3 US Colored	35 Bn. VA

Robinson's Sharps Carbines

11 VA Cav.

Smith Carbines

Cavalry	
U.S.	C.S.
1 CT	2 NC
7 IL	7 VA
11 IL	11 VA
9 KY	12 VA
1 MA	35 Bn. VA
10 NY	
7 PA	

Spencer Carbines

Cavalry	9 MI
U.S.	2 NJ
6 IL	3 NJ
9 IL	1 NY Vet
12 IL	2 NY
8 IN	5 NY
2 IA	19 NY
4 IA	2 OH
2 MA	3 OH
4 MA	5 OH
1 MI	11 OH
2 MI	12 OH
4 MI	7 PA
5 MI	15 PA
6 MI	2 WI
7 MI	4 US

Starr Carbines

Cavalry
U.S.

1 AR	24 NY
13 IL	19 PA
9 IA	Merrills Horse
5 KS	
3 MI	
11 MO	
12 MO	
1 NY Vet	
12 NY	

Double-barrel Shotguns

C.S.
15 AR
24 Bn. GA Cav
8 TX Cav
11 TX Cav
14 VA Cav

Adams Revolvers

C.S.
1 VA Cav

Colt Navy Revolvers

Cavalry
U.S.
2 IL   4 US
13 IL
1 IN   C.S.
5 KS   8 TX
6 KS   1 VA
7 KS   7 VA
9 KS   11 VA
1 ME   12 VA
1 NY   14 VA
11 OH   17 VA
1 RI   34 Bn. VA
                             35 Bn. VA

Colt Army Revolvers

Cavalry
U.S.
2 CA   2 US
1 CT   3 US
1 DE   Loudon Rgrs VA
4 IL
8 IL   C.S.
6 KY   1 VA
10 KY   7 VA
1 ME   11 VA
2 NY   12 VA
3 NY   14 VA
6 NY   15 VA
7 NY   17 VA
8 NY   34 Bn. VA
9 NY   35 Bn. VA
11 NY
1 NJ
4 OH
1 PA
2 PA
8 PA
11 PA
1 US

Joslyn Revolvers

Cavalry   7 IA
U.S.   7 KS
16 IL   1 MO
3 IA   5 OH

Kerr Revolvers

Cavalry   7 VA
C.S.   11 VA
24 Bn. GA   12 VA
8 TX   35 Bn. VA

Lefaucheux Revolvers

Cavalry   5 KS
U.S.   6 KY
Dakota Terr.   8 MO
5 IL   9 MO State Mil.
2 KS   1 WI

Remington Navy Revolvers

Cavalry   3 IA
U.S.   8 IA
1 IN   9 KY
9 IL   3 MO
13 IL   9 OH
2 IA   17 PA

Remington Army Revolvers

Cavalry   14 KS
U.S.   9 KY
1 DC   2 MA
3 IL   2 MI
2 IN   6 OH
4 IA   10 OH
9 IA   17 PA
9 KS   3 TN
11 KS   1 VT

Savage Revolvers

Cavalry
U.S.   10 MO State Mil
5 KS   12 MO State Mil
7 MO   1 WI
2 MO State Mil   2 WI
3 MO State Mil
4 MO State Mil   C.S.
5 MO State Mil   11 TX
6 MO State Mil   7 VA
7 MO State Mil   34 Bn. VA
8 MO State Mil   35 Bn. VA

Starr Army Revolvers			Whitney Revolvers	
Cavalry	1 NH		Cavalry	
U.S.	2 OH		U.S.	3 NY
4 IA	4 OH		7 IL	7 OH
1 MO	14 PA		2 IA	5 PA
7 MO State Mil	1 WI		9 KS	11 PA
			1 MS	5 TN

Bibliography and Suggested Reading

Albaugh, William A., III and Simmons, Edward N., *Confederate Arms,* The Stackpole Company, Harrisburg, PA, 1957.

Edwards, William B., *Civil War Guns,* The Stackpole Company, Harrisburg, 1962.

Coggins, Jack, *Arms and Equipment of the Civil War,* Doubleday & Company, Garden City, NY, 1962.

Flayderman, Norm, *Flayderman's Guide to Antique American Firearms...and their Values,* 4th Edition, DBI Books, Northbrook, IL, 1987.

Fuller, Claud E., *The Rifled Musket,* Bonanza Books, New York, 1958.

Hicks, Major James E., *French Military Weapons,* N. Flayderman & Co., New Milford, CT, 1964.

Hill, Richard T. and Anthony, William E., *Confederate Longarms and Pistols,* Hill and Anthony Publishers, Charlotte, NC, 1978.

Lord, Francis A., *Civil War Collector's Encyclopedia,* The Stackpole Company, Harrisburg, 1965.

Marcot, Roy M., *Spencer Repeating Arms,* Northwood Heritage Press, Irvine, CA, 1983.

McAulay, John D., *Carbines of the Civil War,* Pioneer Press, Union City, TN, 1981.

McAulay, John D., *Civil War Breechloading Rifles,* Andrew Mowbray Inc., Lincoln, RI, 1987.

_____, *The Ordnance Manual for the Use of the Officers of the United States Army,* J.B. Lippincott & Co., Philadelphia, 1862.

Patterson, C. Meade and De Marco, Cuddy, Jr., *Civil War Small Arms,* National Rifle Assoc., Washington, DC.

Roads, C.H., *The British Soldier's Firearm, 1850-1864,* Herbert Jenkins Ltd., London, 1964.

Sellers, Frank, *Sharps Firearms,* Beinfeld Publishing Inc., N. Hollywood, CA, 1978.

Smith, Gene P. and Curtis, Chris C., *The Pinfire System,* Bushman-Brashaw Publishing Co., San Francisco, CA, 1983.

Swayze, Nathan L., *'51 Colt Navies,* Gun Hill Publishing Co., Yazoo City, MS, 1967.

Thomas, Dean S., *Ready...Aim...Fire! Small Arms Ammunition in the Battle of Gettysburg,* Thomas Publications, Gettysburg, PA, 1981.

Todd, Frederick P., *American Military Equipage, 1851-1872,* The Company of Military Historians, Providence, RI, 1974.

Wilson, R.L., *The Colt Heritage,* Simon and Schuster, New York, 1939.